THE IRON-BLUE VAULT

ATTILA JÓZSEF, 1934

Attila József

THE
IRON-BLUE VAULT
Selected Poems

translated by
ZSUZSANNA OZSVÁTH
& FREDERICK TURNER

BLOODAXE BOOKS

ISBN: 1 85224 503 4

First published 1999 by
Bloodaxe Books Ltd,
P.O. Box 1SN,
Newcastle upon Tyne NE99 1SN.

Bloodaxe Books Ltd acknowledges
the financial assistance of Northern Arts.

ACKNOWLEDGEMENTS
This translation was supported by the Frankfurt '99
Programme Office of the Hungarian Ministry of Culture.

The photographs are reproduced by kind permission
of the Magyar Irodalmi Múzeum, Budapest.

Cover printing by J. Thomson Colour Printers Ltd, Glasgow.

Printed in Great Britain by
Cromwell Press Ltd, Trowbridge, Wiltshire.

He who would a piper be
must go to hell unswervingly;
only in that place may he know
how he should make the pipes to blow.

Hungarian folksong, used by Attila József
as the epigraph to Medvetánc *(Bear Dance),*
a collection of his poems

CONTENTS

ATTILA JÓZSEF, 1924

'SUN-BEDAZZLED, DREAM-AFFLICTED': THE SEARCH FOR ATTILA JÓZSEF

Zsuzsanna Ozsváth

Attila József is one of the greatest Hungarian lyric poets of the 20th century. The roll and resonance of his verse are known to virtually every school child in his country, the turns of his poetic speech have renewed, and his shamanic voice has added new echoes to the creative resources of Hungarian language and culture. Yet such poetic sweep and the deep urgency out of which it rises are never restricted to one language or culture: rather they are of vital, universal significance. They attract other people's cultural affinities and affect and challenge worldwide audiences. It is the purpose of this translation to give József's lyrical verses a full sense in English.[1]

Such an introduction must also involve, however, a discussion of both the sociocultural context out of which these poems arose and their connection with the arduous personal evolution of the author himself. Born in Budapest in 1905, Attila József committed suicide in 1937. His life and fate offer more compelling themes to ponder than the great realists of the 19th and 20th century could handle in their fictions: destitution, abuse, humiliation, political engagement, alienation, mental illness, tragic love, genius, poetic inspiration and suicide. They also reflect the extraordinary upheavals that shaped his time: World War I, Communism, Fascism, the Depression and the catastrophic developments in the Third Reich. And they include his response to these upheavals – among others, his indictment of Hungary's Right-conservative leadership and his refusal to become part of the radical-populist, anti-Semitic literary ideology that dominated a large portion of Hungary's intellectual life in the interwar period. He sided with another group, accused by the former of having 'Jewish left-wing sympathies', a group that had in reality a diverse membership, ranging from Western-style liberals to Marxists. József belonged among the latter, at least for awhile.

But he was misled neither by power nor orthodoxy. As he perceived the cataclysmic potential of the Third Reich (he was, by the way, not Jewish), so he discerned the violence of the Soviet scene. Solitary and anguished, he kept on fighting against the extreme pressures these systems exerted on his country's intellectual circles, a struggle which separated him from most of his colleagues, on the Left and Right alike. His commitment to his vision of the truth took its toll. In fact, the more he felt rejected, the more absorbed he became in his own psychological turmoil, with the latter developing into the central issue of his life and poetry. He tried to counter his alienation by remaining preoccupied with the country's large political crises. He shared the despair and frustration generated by the Depression, and persisted in recording the social conflict between the elite and the lower classes. He also observed Hungary's increasing vulnerability to the rising militant, nationalist tide, and attempted to change it by creating images other than the popular ones born out of fear and xenophobia. With the intensity of his poetic imagination – boldly, dramatically, and perspicaciously – he drew a picture of a world in which all people of the Danubian nations would recognise themselves as part of the same fate and geography, thus finding their common peace and purpose among the nations of Europe. As his speaker maintains in the visionary poem 'By the Danube' (1936):

> I am the world, what is and what is fading,
> all nations that contend on hill and plain,
> I die with every conqueror, invading,
> and suffer with the conquered in their pain.
> My heart swells with them, the past's helpless debtor:
> Árpád, Werbőczi, Dózsa and Zalán,[2]
> Romanian, Turk, Slovakian, and Tatar,
> gentle future of each Hungarian!
>
> ...I must have work. Would it were task sufficient
> that one confess the past. The ripples of
> the Danube, that is future, past, and present,
> fondle and hold each other in their love.
> Our forebears' struggle, with its strife and slaughter,
> remembrance melts and renders into peace:
> our common labours now to set in order,
> were pains enough to be our masterpiece.

Of course, Attila József's life reveals itself not only in his political insights, intellectual discoveries and inner struggles, but, most important, in his unsurpassed, profoundly musical poetic oeuvre that integrates what Fred Turner calls the 'ancient grace', the riches of metre and the exactions of formal perfection, with both sharp intellectual analysis and the extraordinary sensitivities of the modern mind and psyche. An ancient magician's passion, madness, and illumination generate here lines and cadences of lovely shapeliness and melodic perfection, which, in turn, bring to the surface with a rolling ease the most personal childhood hurts, the young man's breathtaking flights of fancy, or the burning cultural, moral issues of the period.

10

ABOVE: *József family, Budapest, 1908: Attila, Etus, Jolán & Mrs Borbála József.*
BELOW: *Attila József, around 1920.*

Attila József with his sister Etus, Makó, Hungary, 1923.

We must keep in mind, however, that the poet's life was over-whelmed by hardship, from its beginning. His mother Borbála Pőcze left her hometown at the age of 15 to try her luck as a domestic maid in the capital. His father Áron József, of Romanian origins, appeared to have been an easy-going young man, who made his living as an unskilled labourer in a soap factory. The two met, took to one another, and had several children (some of whom died in infancy) before they married. Still, with or without a marriage licence, the young couple's life was far from happy. Cut loose from their roots, they were ill-equipped both economically and socially for raising children. Like the rest of the poor in the slums of Budapest, they floundered from job to job, from apartment to apartment in the outskirts of the capital. At first, Áron was just chasing fun, trying to escape the responsibilities his family posed. After a while, however, he started to spend his nights at his lovers' homes; or he hid out in nearby taverns, going home drunk and angry, so that his wife had to lock the trembling children in a closet to save them from his rage. One day he disappeared forever. Attila, the youngest of three surviving siblings, was three years old. Never quite capable of dealing with this trauma, the boy remained pre-occupied with the role his father played in his life for as long as he lived:

> Áron József got me;
> who beyond the Endless Sea,
> soapmaker, forgot me;
> now he mows the pungent hay.
>
> ('Áron József Got Me', 1928)[3]

Áron's desertion of his family had grave consequences: the weight of the family fell on Borbála alone. And this was a burden the young woman just couldn't carry. Her wages were insufficient for the support of the little boy and his two sisters, Jolán and Etus, her mothering skills stretched to the limit. The four of them moved first into a rented room, then into ever cheaper quarters, until they arrived at the basement of a slum house, sleeping together at night on a bedbug-ridden mattress on the floor. Realising after a while that there was no reprieve, Borbála gave up the struggle. She con-tacted the National Child Protection League, letting them place Etus, seven, and Attila, five years old, in the care of foster parents. The foster mother, Mrs Gombai, came by herself to pick up the children from a League-sponsored camp, returning with them to Öcsöd, a small town in the countryside. Themselves peasant small-holders whose income barely provided a subsistence standard of living, the Gombais were in dire need of cheap helping hands. Now they had what they wanted. The children worked for nothing: Etus in the house and Attila as a swineherd. He would never forget the pain he suffered in that house. As he remembers it in 'Medallions' (1927-28), a strangely surrealistic, magical song:

On the frail drop of dew a dust-mote crawls,
I cover with my hands pants full of holes,
the little swineherd weeps and hugs alone
his pied piglet enchanted into stone –

Of course, it was not the new vocation, but the break-up of his family that shattered the boy's life. The brutal treatment he received from his foster parents aggravated his anguish. For Gombai beat Attila constantly, while his wife watched the torture indifferently. And the boy's abuse was not restricted to physical blows alone. His foster parents decided to change his name. 'Ascertaining' in a discusssion with their next-door neighbors that there was no one in the world who could possibly be called Attila, the couple renamed the child Pisti (Stevie). Now he had lost not only his home and his parents, but also his name. Except for Etus, the five-year-old had lost everyone he loved, everything that supported his identity.

During the two years the children spent at Öcsöd, their mother visited them only once. Could she not afford the cost of such a trip? Was it her sense of guilt that held her back? Or did the separation hurt her so much that she couldn't bear to see the misery of her little ones? We will never know. What we know, though, is that when she arrived in Öcsöd after more than a year of separation, Attila, rigid and wide-eyed with terror, ran away from her, only to sob disconsolately each time he caught her look during that visit; and that when she left, the six-year-old broke out in a sudden rage, pulled a knife, and attacked his sister Etus. In vain did he rage or rend his own flesh, however; he had to stay in Öcsöd for yet another year. Then, suddenly, the nightmare ended: their mother picked them up and returned with them to Budapest where the family was reunited.

But was it really? The idyll of the past that the little boy had so desperately yearned for did not return. The hand-to-mouth struggle to raise her family and the raw fear in her bones that she could not do it wore Borbála down. Working seven days a week, she was exhausted at night, incapable of communicating with her children. In fact, she fell into a deep depression: at times, just sitting around in the room, weeping in anguish. She also attempted suicide several times. Once it was the eight-year-old Attila, recovering at home

14

from a nearly fatal pneumonia, who held her down and stopped her from jumping out of the window.

A year later, it was the boy's turn. Angry at Jolán, who had slapped his face for stealing cigarettes from her purse, he decided to kill himself. He drank what he thought was poison (sodium hydroxide, an alkaline compound used by his mother for bleaching laundry). Wishing to get back at Jolán and everyone else in the world who had wronged him, he let Etus know what he had done. The effect was jolting: although the little girl didn't understand the reasons for her brother's action, she did perceive his despair. She took the boy in her arms, carrying him to the caretaker's flat. The news spread like wildfire in the neighbourhood; a large number of women gathered around him, and his mother rushed to his bedside. It was soon discovered that what he had drunk was not sodium hydroxide, but rather a bottle of harmless starch. He didn't die. Still, the event traumatised his family: his sisters shook; and his frenzied mother carried the child around in her arms, kissing and caressing him throughout the night. But her kisses and caresses didn't allay Attila's anguished yearning for love; rather, they intensified it. The idea of suicide became from then on his life's companion. In the years to come, he tried to kill himself again and again, until he succeeded at last.

From the time he was eight, and Etus, ten, the children worked, helping their mother to support the family. They scrubbed floors, carried baskets for other people at the market-place, and sold water as well as home-made toy windmills at the cinema where Jolán worked in the box office. As for the family's fuel supply, it was provided by Attila, who spent his nights near the train stations, stealing coal from the arriving coal wagons. Yet despite the children's desperate efforts to make money, the family continued to live in misery: their diet remained insufficient, their housing overcrowded, and their clothing inadequate. Etus and Attila had to leave again. This time the Children's Protection League placed them in Monor, in yet another foster home in the countryside. Luckily, this sojourn was shorter than the first one; their mother took them back to Budapest within a few months. By now, the fifteen-year-old Jolán had married a young man and let her family move with her to a better apartment. Still, their lot didn't change significantly: they continued to be besieged by poverty and bad fortune. These pressures undermined Borbála's psychic resistance; she started to whip her children, especially Attila, hard enough to draw blood. Once she attacked him with a rolling-pin for surreptitiously eating all the sweet rolls she had baked, and beat him to within an inch of his life. A neighbour came to his rescue. But the memory of the beating and the desperate guilt that arose in its wake remained active in the young man's mind, festering in him throughout his life. As he complained twenty years later: 'I would so much like to reverse my gobbling up the sweet rolls'; and then, tortured by pangs of guilt for the ways in which she sacrificed herself for her children's well-being, he added: '[Rather than eating], Mama brought home even her dinner'.[4]

These were hard times for everyone in Hungary. Suffering enormous economic and human losses in the battles of World War I, the country continued to follow an endless, downward spiral. Living conditions deteriorated; food supplies declined. When Attila turned twelve, he had to leave school to help his mother full-time. And now the worst happened. Borbála Pőcze fell ill, her body ravaged by a massive uterine cancer. In and out of hospitals, she stayed at home for ever shorter periods of time.

During the long and chaotic winter months of 1919-20, the country's food and fuel shortages increased the hunger in the cities. Defeated in World War I, weakened by a bad harvest, and threatened by its own seceding minorities, Hungary appeared to be depleted of its last resources, on the brink of collapse. In the course of the coming months, people stood in bread and coal lines sometimes for twenty-four hours at a stretch, only to learn that there was nothing left for them at the end. Starvation became the order of the day. In the course of this year, Attila travelled several times to Szabadszállás, to his mother's relatives in the countryside, bringing food from them back to the family in Budapest. But the journey on which he embarked in November 1919 lasted longer than planned. First of all, it was bitterly cold, so that he was quite happy to stay in the warm and comfortable house of his uncle at Szabadszállás over the Christmas holiday. Second, the country's transportation facilities ran much slower than he had imagined they would. The trains were crowded and stood still at times for days between the stations, on the tracks and in the open fields. When he finally returned to Jolán's apartment on 6 January 1920, only two frightened girls were waiting for him. Their mother had died a few days before. All he could do was visit her graveside. The boy was fourteen years old. Years later, in one of his most dramatic invocations of his mother, 'Late Lament' (1935-36), he tells of the journey to and from Szabadszállás and the hair-raising news he learned upon his arrival:

> I'd gone to Szabadszállás, I remember,
>   the last days of the wars;
> for Budapest lay stricken that November,
> and there was no bread in the city's stores.
> I'd bought potatoes, millet tied in sacking,
> I lay across a train's roof, belly-prone;
> would not take 'no' until I'd got a chicken,
>   but when I came, you'd gone.

But how can one survive such blows to the body and the soul? It is difficult to generalise; and even more difficult to explain Attila József's life and lyrical development in terms of this abuse. Still studying his oeuvre, one feels constantly confronted with the traces, marks, and grafts of these blows; and finds oneself constantly face to face with the impact they made on the poet's creative imagination. As a matter of fact, József's oeuvre manifestly demonstrates that there are deep interconnections between the poet's life and his lyrical imagination, and that his awareness of the link between his abuse and poetic memory is a constituent element of his work. It also reveals that these experiences give his ideation a stark emotionally sharpened context and that they illuminate the ways in which he tried to come to terms with, to humanise, mythologise, and thereby work through the tyrannies of his childhood. Ultimately, then, it is not only József's lyrical tropes but also the process of shaping his own personal life story into poetry and the creation of the legend of his persona, public and private alike, that reflect both his reception of the traumas he had experienced and his attempts at transcending them.

After his mother's death, the boy moved with Etus to the flat of Jolán and her second husband Ödön Makai. But Makai, an intelligent, well-to-do lawyer, felt ill at ease with, even ashamed of, his unpolished, proletarian in-laws. Coming from the upper layers of Hungary's class-conscious bourgeoisie, Makai had never lived before among people from the slums. Thus, despite his liberal interests, he was uncomfortable around the children. Even Jolán, quite sophisticated by now, felt torn between her past and the world of her husband. She distanced herself from her own siblings, maintaining that her name wasn't Jolán but Lucie and that she wasn't their real sister but an acquaintance who had come to live with them for a while. And this was not meant as a joke. When visitors came to the couple, the children were introduced as servants, with their activities restricted to preparing dinner and washing dishes. This was more than Attila could take. He left his sisters and brother-in-law for a tug-boat on the Danube. Scrubbing the decks during the summer for a pittance, he wore himself out with hard work. This endeavour was followed by yet another attempt at finding a home for himself, away from his family. He joined a Catholic seminary, but left within two weeks. He then decided to take a series of supplementary examinations that would allow him to continue his studies in a gymnasium setting, necessary for a person who wished to enroll eventually in an institute of higher learning.

With Makai pulling some strings, Attila was accepted in a boarding school at Makó, a town in the Hungarian lowlands near the southern border. He became a student once again; and an excellent one at that. He not only made outstanding grades, but also discovered his gift for poetry. Starting to publish, he earned the admiration of his teachers and fellow students alike. The boy was delighted, indeed, bedazzled by so much attention. His happiness was short-lived, however. As soon as he published a love poem in the local newspaper, a scandal broke out: everyone seemed to know that the muse of these tropes was the daughter of the school principal. The faculty was outraged, censuring him for his audacity, forbidding him to publish anything without permission. Attila felt expelled from paradise: rejected, unloved, reduced to nothing. He made another suicide attempt. This time it was serious: he swallowed a bottle of aspirin – sixty tablets he had collected one by one over a long period of time. 'Saved' once more, he left the boarding school. To obtain a certificate of graduation was not his goal any more; he decided to dedicate his life to poetry.

He even found people who helped him in this endeavour; among them was Gyula Juhász, one of the greatest Hungarian poets of the epoch. Praising the young man highly, Juhász was instrumental in the publication of the seventeen-year-old's first volume of poetry *The Beggar of Beauty* (1922). But József's success as a promising poet notwithstanding, he needed a job. Although he found one as a bank clerk and soon another as a book salesman, he wasn't very successful in either field; thus, he remained dependent on his mentors as well as on his family. After yet another suicide attempt, he went ahead and took the necessary high school examination that fulfilled the requirement for his graduation at the István Werböczy Gymnázium in Budapest. In the autumn of 1924, he enrolled in the Ferenc József University at Szeged. Majoring in French and Hungarian, he intended to become a secondary school teacher.

But adversities kept plaguing the young man's life. In the summer of 1924, he was taken to court for his poem 'Rebelling Christ' on charges of blasphemy. Of course, the charges had no basis, but were simply part of the continuing witch-hunts the semi-Fascist Horthy régime were launching against 'Communist agents' and 'Jewish infiltrators'. Although Attila fitted neither of these categories (he became interested in Communist ideas at a later point in his life), the free spirit blowing through his poems sent a danger signal to the watchdogs of the system, determined to eradicate what they defined as 'Leftist attempts' at undermining the values of 'Christian' Hungary. At the trial he was found guilty and not only sentenced to eight months in prison but also fined a significant sum of money. He lived under the pressure of this sentence until he was acquitted by an appeals court.

Then, he was assaulted anew. The blow came from one of his teachers, Antal Horger, Professor of Philology at the School of Humanities. Attila's new poem 'With a Pure Heart' (March 1925) outraged Horger. He found it both immoral and sacrilegious, undermining the values of Hungarian youth. Censuring József in front of two witnesses, he announced that the young man would never be able to obtain a job as a schoolteacher in Hungary. The threat shook him; what would he do instead? As he remembered the scene years later in his bitter-brash mock-song 'For My Birthday' (April 1937):

> ... Herr College Chancellor
> Showed me the outside of the door:
> > mocktor
> > Doctor.
>
> It was a short sharp shock for sure,
> my 'father' poem got its cure;
> > his word
> > and sword,
>
> that saved the fatherland from me,
> evoked my spirit and set free
> > its name
> > and flame.
>
> 'As long as I have any say
> you'll not teach here a single day' –
> > bibble-
> > babble.

But József not only understood the implications of Horger's threat; by 1937, the time he composed this 'birthday' poem, he also recognised his own significance in the culture of his country:

> If Mr Antal Horger's pleased,
> our poet's grammar-study ceased –
> > folly's
> > jollies –

no high school, but a nation I,
although he like not, by and by
    shall teach,
    shall teach.

As his academic career came to an end in Szeged, the young man left Hungary for Austria and enrolled at the University of Vienna. Taking classes in art history, philosophy and French, he remained for a year in the Austrian capital. He also met a number of artists and intellectuals among the Hungarian emigrants who had fled to Vienna from the pogroms staged in their country first by the counter-revolutionary Army, then by the police of the new Hungarian state, against Jews and Communists. Many of these refugees remained deeply involved in the art scene in Budapest; so that they had known József's poetry even before he arrived and befriended him during his sojourn in Vienna. Still, this exciting exchange of ideas notwithstanding, he had a hard life during that year. He lived in abject poverty: working as a janitor and selling newspapers to earn the bare minimum. At times, he received help from some of his friends and Makai, who let him go to Paris after the year was over. This was an opportunity of enormous significance. Paris has always been the city of pilgrimage for Hungarian poets and thinkers; now Attila was given the opportunity to follow in their footsteps. He matriculated at the Sorbonne and took classes for two semesters, studying logic, aesthetics, Romanticism, and a number of other subjects. He read the works of a great many authors, such as Ronsard, Balzac, La Fontaine, Prevost and Victor Hugo; and he also learned French well enough to compose poetry in it. The new avant-garde journal, *L'Esprit Nouveau* even published one of his poems, placing it next to the works of such internationally known authors as Hans Arp, Céline, Walter Gropius, F.T. Marinetti and Tristan Tzara. In France, József became interested in political thought as well; while studying the works of Hegel, Marx, and Lenin, he joined the Union Anarchiste-Communiste. In the summer of 1927, he returned to Budapest.

While these years of peregrination and immersion in foreign cultures were central to the young man's intellectual-artistic development, opening him up to new worlds of thinking and new languages, they didn't, and of course couldn't, teach him the basics of how to earn a living. After all that time, he still had obtained no diploma, created no business, found for himself no occupation or trade. What would he do? Coming back to Budapest, he enrolled at the Péter Pázmány University but dropped out after the second semester.

Yet the problem grew: either he had to find a job that clashed with his desire to write poetry or else remain sentenced to the world of destitution, forever penniless, forever humiliated. He tried out one job after the other, but couldn't resolve the dilemma for as long as he lived.

While painfully self-conscious of his precarious status in the world and constantly beleaguered by economic necessities, József tried to find his place in the Hungarian literary circles. He became friends with Gyula Illyés and József Erdélyi, two aspiring young poets; and he met the literary crowd of Budapest in the city's cafés, where they sat all day, drinking coffee, working and arguing with one another. He also started to publish regularly in some of the country's major journals, even in its most prestigious one, *Nyugat* [Occident]. The signs of his genius were obvious by now, as his poetry began to show its power and spectacular beauty.

To arrive at this level of perfection, however, he had to make hard choices and undergo a remarkable development. Initially, the roots of József's lyrics went back to the older generation of the great Hungarian poets of the 20th century, to Ady, Juhász, Kosztolányi, and Babits; while the deepest sources of his verse-making sprang from the nineteenth: from the works of Petőfi, even Vörösmarty. Still, while aware of this formidable legacy, the young man, as every young artist, started to crave the new. He locked his eyes on the national and international avant-garde, which showed right then, an extraordinarily broad range of different styles and modes of expression. Among them, in poetry, free verse emerged as the most frequented structure of the modernists. Many of them found this irregular metric pattern as the best means for expressing the dissonant tensions and radical enigmas of the modern mind. Listening to and participating in these literati's political and aesthetic debates, József imbibed the problems, tensions, and crises through which his generation was passing and was uncertain for a while how to deal with the new inspirations and constrictions involved in the practice of his craft. First of all, he believed, like so many literati of the time, in the high role poetry would play in the creation of a new and better world and in the poet's task of educating tomorrow's youth. But this line of thinking often conflicted with his notions of aesthetic choices and the complexities of his work. Small wonder: the problem was loaded with the tension. On the one hand, he was aware of both the Hungarian strong stress on the first syllable of the word and the distinct metre that thus appears in both the spoken and the lyrical language of the Magyars. And he also knew that Hungarian poetry has embraced a great variety of enormously diverse patterns of poetic speech in its long and distinguished history, that, in fact, it is capable of accommodating the verse practice of other languages, such as the Germanic and Romance, old and new alike. On the other, however, he didn't want to continue weaving the strings of the past, but rather create a new pattern of being. He decided to join the avant-garde and work for a new and better future.

Measuring his verse-making at the time against that of others on the national scene, Andor Németh observed that 'Attila wavered between [two styles]: the styles of Erdélyi and Kassák'.[5] What this comparison means more concretely involves the two extremes of the Hungarian world of poetry in the 20s and 30s: the constructivist, dadaist, and expressionist influence of the great Hungarian modernist Kassák and the musical, peasant-oriented, folksong-inspired approach of Erdélyi, pulling József into two opposing directions.

If he wavered in the mid-20s, by 1927, he found his own approach, unmatched by others. Rather than giving up the achievements of the past, he appropriated and perfected an enormous variety of classical, symbolist, and modernist structures, eclectically mixing and changing them with fiendish virtuosity. Although his verse had always tended to communicate through sonorities and incantatory metre, now he developed a genre, the thrust of which is anchored in the music of magic charms, spells, lullabies, nursery rhymes, and the Hungarian folksong. As Bartók's *Cantata Profana* echoes the ancient sounds of the country's Asian heritage, creating effects that are new in European music, so do József's rhythmic patterns and melodic lines produce a voice and an effect heretofore unknown in Hungarian poetry:

> Like unto a stag I fled,
> soft grief made my eyes to smart.
> Forest-gnawing wolves unfed
> hunt each other in my heart.
>
> ('Grief', 1930)

And in infinite variations, new keys and new structures emerge in a number of poems. As, for example, in the air-light, tender-sweet movement of the 'The Kings of Bethlehem' (1929):

> Flushing-blushing Mary-girl, Mary-girl!
> Blessed mother, flower and pearl,
>   through her tears in showers falling,
>   scarcely sees her Jesus-darling,
>   hears the shepherds' drum and piper,
>   but the baby needs his supper.

Dearest kings so fine and bright,
now I wish you all good night!

Also the melodic line and the arcane, tensely rhythmic merry-go-rounds of 'The Last of Seven' (1932) spring from this lineage:

Mortal dweller, may your mother
bear you seven times together!
once within a house that's burning,
once in floods, the icefloes churning,
once in bedlam, yelling, yearning,
once in a wheatfield's soft turning,
once in cloisters bell-intoning,
once stied with pigs in grunts and groaning.
What though these six cry out to heaven?
You shall be the last of seven!

With his creative power surging by the end of the 20s, József longed for soul-mates and colleagues: he needed their attention, he needed their support. While reaching out to a number of them, he needed perhaps no one's respect more pressingly and sought no one's attention more consciously and more intensely than that of Mihály Babits, editor-in-chief of *Occident*, and one of the great poets of Hungary's golden age of poetry.

But the young man didn't succeed in forging a relationship with Babits. Athough Babits published some of József's poems, he didn't seem to have time for, or a particular interest in, the young man himself. At least, this is the conclusion Attila drew. And he was perhaps not wrong. Why? Hard to know; there are mere conjectures. It seems plausible, however, that the vastly different life experiences of the two poets sufficed to create a wall separating them in an almost natural way from one another. Their views on the role of art and culture, and therefore their own self-definition and concept of their place in the world, clashed quite powerfully.

Tired of violence and the passionate actions that followed passionate ideas, Babits had withdrawn from politics ever since the early 20s. In contrast, József, having just arrived on the literary scene toward the end of the decade, threw himself directly into the fray of radical ideas. Branded by his degrading experience of poverty, he revealed an almost natural affinity with extreme political issues, and a clamouring dislike for the élite, with its roots in a deeply divided, hierarchical society. After a brief involvement with the populist movement, he turned to the Communists. Committed to changing the world, he believed that it was the task of intellectuals and artists to bring about the moral transformation of society. As so many poets before him, he believed in the historical significance of his vision and in the reality of his cosmic insights. Such beliefs echo in the effusive invocation of the speaker in 'On the Edge of the City' (Spring 1933):

> The poet – the word may rattle on his lips,
> but he (the engineer
> who serves the magic of the given world),
> seeing the future clear,
> as you without, so he within constructs
> a new harmonic sphere.

Although Babits, too, believed that poets occupy a central position in culture, he didn't want to listen to their voice in the battle cry of the Revolution. He had heard that already in 1919 when an impressive number of avant-garde artists and poets declared themselves willing to resound the exhortatory message of the Communist régime. Small wonder that Babits, who was slandered for years by official Hungary for his political envolvement with pacifist circles during the war and for his acceptance of a professorship during the incumbency of Béla Kún's Soviet government, wished to extricate himself from that history. Turning his back on the past, he had no sympathy for young radicals who believed in the necessity of overthrowing the system. In fact, the older he grew, the more he rejected both the politicisation of life and poetry and the division of art into progressive and decadent realms. Pitting literature against radicalism, he maintained that high culture was the only possible antidote for our declining civilisation. And he tried everything in his power as a poet, as an editor of *Occident*, and as a curator of Hungary's most prestigious literary foundation, to emphasise this critical position.

That his "priestly" functions, high power, and aesthetic outlook gave him an enormous edge over the young Hungarian literati and that the latter resented him for his power goes without saying. But most artists of the Hungarian literary scene didn't oppose Babits; partly because they were aware of the unsurpassed work he produced; partly, however, because he was an honorable man, and most people knew that. His opponents sprang predominantly from the ranks of the radicals: the far Right, and, at times, the Left.

But the blow Attila brazenly levelled at Babits was hard, swift, and unexpected. It aimed at the older man's newly published volume of poetry: *Gods Die; Man Lives*. Poking fun at both Babits's poetic ideas and his versification, József dipped his pen in poison: 'In [Babits's poems],' he wrote, 'form and content, artistic form and poetic content, avoid one another as mutual conjugal murderers, each suspecting Sherlock Holmes in the other.'[6] And after tearing apart all, the poems' metric order, symbolism, metaphors, images, and lyrical statements, the young man closed his essay contemptuously: 'If Mihály Babits were still a fledgling poet, and if this volume were his first one, I would have written that some of his lines indubitably indicate talent. But the book in its entirety casts doubt on the development of such talent.'[7] The Hungarian literary community held its breath, for the attack was as irrational as it was undeserved. Why did József do it? Perhaps because he wished to defend his friend Ignotus who had had a dramatic clash with Babits a short while before. Perhaps because the young man wanted to show the public that no matter what, he would always address the 'truth'? Acccording to József's mentor Hatvany, what drove this essay was nothing else but self-destruction. Attila '...wrote against Babits in such a way as if he had written against himself, cursing with each word what he loved the most: Babits's poetry, Babits's person.'[8] Is it possible that what triggered Attila's outbreak involved an ancient trauma fomenting for years, before it exploded? Could this attack be seen as a displaced reaction to the events of the past? As an outburst of the son rejected by his father? Or could one take it as the expression of a generational wall forever separating the young and the old from one another? The impatience of a young man with the world of yesterday? It's hard to know. What we know, however, is that a few months later, Attila did it again; this time, in a lyrical composition, entitled 'On a Poet' (April 1930). The first stanza alone reveals the enormity of the attack:

> Yapping jackal, croaking raven,
> shamed, the prince of sneers
> blurts his song, the filthy craven,
> master but of years.
> Less than a leech, he mocks his psalms
> who dreams not of his hothouse palms.

Literary Budapest was petrified. However heroic Attila might have appeared for the moment in his own eyes for having dared the undarable, he came to regret it bitterly. As his beautiful, philosophical poem to Babits, 'Self-devouring...', three years later (June 1933) testifies: 'Self-devouring, haggard Virtue! I have hurt you.' Trying to explain both his affection for and distance from Babits, the young man closes the poem with a tender, woe-filled stanza:

> And there, confused,
> for a time I idly mused
> how after all we might
> have been good friends, how on this night
> we could be bound for some café,
> what I would say, what you would say,
> how, stirring tea, we might pursue
> the good, the beautiful, the true,

and talk of literary trends
and such important human odds and ends;
how I would mark the pregnant words you'd say,
which you judiciously would weigh,
alluding to your long experience:
how I'd be carried off with passion,
how you while adding: 'please don't take offence' –
would raise your older hand in admonition,
as fathers do,
and I'd be vexed, but would not tell you so.

Not even this poem could melt the ice, though. The damage was done. As Andor Németh maintained: 'With this disrespectful invective, directed against the curator of the Baumgarten Foundation, Attila removed himself from the ranks of the talented, worthy of support.'[9] And Babits himself remarked in an essay four years after the young man's suicide: 'There were authors about whom I couldn't write for personal reasons. It was poor Attila József himself who made this difficult for me.'[10] The affair undermined József's relationship not only with Babits, however, but also with several other literati in Babits' circle, revolving around *Occident*. And worse: although he received over the years one or two small awards from the Baumgarten Foundation, he never won its Grand Prize, a raw wound József lived with until the end of his life.[11]

If Babits didn't immediately recognise the young man's talent and significance as a poet, to what extent did the rest of the Hungarian literary world know who he was? Of course, a number of people opposed József for his Leftist stance alone. And the others? Some of them knew. But we must not forget that at a time of such political tension, in such a din of embittered cultural battles, when so much emotion and so much excellence vied for attention, it must have been difficult to step back, sort out, and measure talent against talent. Indeed, while torn by internecine conflicts, the Hungarian world of letters in the early thirties was teeming with genius. Of the giants of the past Babits, Kosztolányi, Juhász, Kassák, Móricz, Füst and Karinthy were still around. In the ranks of the young, such talents as Márai, Illyés, Radnóti, József and Weöres appeared, each demanding attention. And, then, there were, of course, scores of other names, such as those of the widely celebrated, popular playwrights Heltai and Molnár, in addition to a wide selection of people involved in drama, history or literary criticism. It had to take some time before József could be fully recognised.

Attila's struggle against the establishment, his early experience, and his self-image of subsisting on the margins of society only reinforced his sense of insecurity and fear of rejection. While part of every aspect of his personhood, these strains manifested themselves most clearly in his relationship with women. By the time the 23-year-old met Márta Vágó in the spring of 1928, the conflict had already crystallised.

By no means a newcomer to affairs of the heart, Attila hadn't yet burnt himself in any of them, nor had he been transformed by them. His experience with Márta that year, however, had dimensions different from all previous relationships. Young, beautiful, interesting, and highly intelligent, she came from a well-to-do, highly respected Jewish family, whose house was a favourite meeting place for young liberals, artists, and intellectuals, conducting passionate discussions about the moral, philosophical, scientific, and aesthetic issues of the day. Among them were such people as the Polányi brothers, Géza Róheim, and Karl Mannheim, who would each become world-renowned a few years later, and such literati as Ignotus, Illyés, Aladár Komlós, and András Komor, each of whom played a significant role in Hungarian literature or literary criticism. This was the first time that Attila had ever been part of such a varied and outstanding group of intellectuals, of such a generous, beautiful, and free-spirited environment.

While he enjoyed meeting and talking with most of these people, including Márta's brilliant father and the rest of her family, he and Márta became especially interested in one another. Out of this interest a passion developed, which neither of them had known or could have imagined before. And the more they were together, the deeper their love, the deeper their happiness. For a short while, it appeared as if Attila had succeeded in leaving behind his fears and insecurities. But this was only an illusion. He hadn't. In fact, the more demanding and urgent their love, the more aware they became of their differing needs and differing expectations. By the beginning of the summer, a mountain of obstacles stood in the way of the pair's happiness: Márta refused Attila's urgings for a sexual relationship, and the young man was unready for a long-term commitment. In love with one another, yet frustrated and tense, the couple watched their best hopes go astray.

The circumstances they were surrounded by also chafed against their raw wounds: Márta's friends and family started to worry about the couple's future. They urged Márta to reconsider her commitment. Their argument was clear and unequivocal: to be tied to Attila meant, they claimed, to be tied to a man who neither could make his living nor would want to have a job. They warned her again and again, maintaining that poverty and homelessness would be her lot if she were to stay with him. Amidst tensions and arguments, by the middle of the summer she decided to follow her family's suggestion and leaving Budapest for a year of study at the London School of Economics. In the meantime, the pair agreed, Attila would either study Economics at the University in Budapest or find a job. Márta's plan materialised; Attila's didn't. They corresponded till the spring of the following year; then their paths parted. Nine years later, they would come together once again. But by then, it was too late: the relationship was rekindled for only a short period of time; then it blew out.

However fraught with frustrations and discord, Attila's passion for Márta inspired a string of beautiful poems, among them such songs as 'I Knew It', 'Pearl' and 'Beads' (Summer 1928). Drawing from nursery rhymes and folksongs, these lyrics touch upon the realm of chant. There is nothing private or eccentric in these pieces, no blurring of the distinction between utterance and aural perception. Concrete words resound the melodic line schemes of ancient music, achieving an existence in the world that borders on that of the song. With 'Beads', József perfected the genre of the song in words, endowing it with enormous powers:

> Beads around your neck aglow,
> frogheads in the lake below.
> Lambkin droppings,
> lambkin droppings in the snow.

> Rose within the moon's halo,
> gold belt round your waist to go.
> Hempen knottings
> knotted round my neck just so.

> Skirted legs so subtly swinging,
> bell-tongue in its bell a-ringing,
> river-mirror
> with two swaying poplars' winging.

> Skirted legs so subtly calling,
> bell-tongue in its bell a-tolling,
> river-mirror
> with the dumb leaves falling, falling.

There is a breathtaking cadence in this poem that combines the rhythms of rocking, nursery rhyme and folksong. These, in turn, invoke images that are as sinister as they are grotesque and surrealistic, manifesting raw emotions, guilt, and the awareness of an impending separation. Central to the process of their development is an inexorable music that brings about the gathering of circular objects and their interweaving into a garland of images: the beads, frogheads, lambkin droppings, the rose, belt, and hempen knottings, the skirt legs, the bell, and the circular poplars, with which the persona has just created both a song and a string of beads.

It was in the autumn of 1930 that the relationship between József and Judit Szántó began. They lived together off and on for the next six years. Judit, a young woman of 20, had already been married twice by the time they met; she also had a daughter, Éva, who was raised by the child's grandparents. Judit had become involved in the Communist movement with her first husband, Antal Hidas, who had left his country and family in 1924 for the Soviet Union. Despite his departure and their subsequent divorce, Judit kept her ties with the illegal Communist Party and took part in its activities and programmes. But she earned her daily bread as an umbrella maker.

Reading her diary, and listening to Attila's friends, mentors and biographers, one must conclude that the relationship between the pair was never very happy. Of course, they were worn down by poverty and the tension created by their constant political disputes. But they also suffered from Attila's rising awareness of his own psychological difficulties and the reality of his deteriorating health. And there were other problems as well: while Attila obviously needed Judit's mothering, he was never passionately in love with her. In fact, she challenged him neither psychically, physically, or intellectually.

Judit, on the other hand, was a woman who defined herself by strong, pro-Soviet views. Hence, she resented everyone who had views that differed from the momentary positions of the Stalin-ruled Communist Party. Regarding her own life as a sacrifice for the Communist Idea, she was contemptuous of everyone who lived without such high ideals. She was also jealous of Attila's friends. 'A bitter woman,' as the writer Németh observed,

> she made umbrellas during the day; at night, with stiff gestures, she kindled the fire, cleaned the house, did the laundry, mended old garments, and dreamed about the day of reckoning, like Brecht's servant in the [*Threepenny Opera*'s] seaman's den. Yes, Judit would have given the same answer to the question of the pirate ship's captain: 'Whom should we kill?' 'All of them.' [12]

Opposing most undertakings of Attila that entailed tasks other than his poetry or political activities, Judit objected to his involvement in psychoanalysis as well.

But as time passed, the political discord that appeared early in their relationship grew, creating more harshness. For the most part, the problem lay in their diverging view of the Communist Party and their own involvement in the movement. Judit embraced

Party discipline, Attila refused to subjugate himself to its whims. At first, their paths had seemed to run parallel to one another. This was in early 1930, after the young man's brief encounter with the spirit and concepts of the liberal reform movement (abundantly manifested in the environment of Márta's friends and family) and his short escapade with the peasant Radical groups. Turning away from both, he decided on another path: to become a speaker and involve himself in the struggle of the suffering masses. He turned to the Marxists, waiting and preparing for the coming revolution.

But he was inexperienced in his dealings with orthodoxy. He liked to argue about and question the rules, regulations and premisses of every intellectual edifice he came across, including his newly appropriated doctrine. And it was precisely this questioning that attracted the suspicion of Hungarian émigrés in the Soviet Union, who read his work in the Party journals and found it dangerous. They attacked him immediately, branding him a 'Fascist Socialist'. These attacks only inspired the young man to ask more questions. In the meantime, he worked hard for the illegal Party, distributing leaflets and organising meetings. He also composed a number of poems, large in scope and visionary, among them 'What Will Become of Him?', 'Night in the Outskirts' and 'On the Edge of the City'. Each of these pieces reveals the suffering and illuminates the beauty and the still unrealised power of the lower classes, suggesting that their creative energy would soon sweep over the world and bring about the long-awaited change. These poems didn't save him from further rejections, though. The emigrés of the Moscow group didn't understand the luminous world the lyrics of József invoked: they simply lacked poetic sensibilities. They didn't hear the beauty of his poetry, its tragic ring, its compelling ideas. Their senses dulled by Stalin's zealous, boring, sycophantic political culture, they simply appropriated the patterns of the Party's attacks, searching for 'enemies' among the Revolution's most loyal supporters. Hence, they continued their assaults on Attila. This had consequences: Attila couldn't take the pressure; neither could he shrug his shoulders. He felt betrayed by his highest hopes. Where would he now find solace?

Judit didn't understand what happened. Out of touch with reality, her diary reveals nothing but ambivalence. She didn't wish to question the coherence of the Party doctrine; nor could she control Attila's intolerance to Soviet's totalitarianism or his rejection of its orthodoxy. The clamour of the dispute between him and the minions of Moscow was raised to a shrill pitch when it became known that two young Hungarian writers, Gyula Illyés and Lajos Nagy, were invited to the First Congress of the Soviet Writers Association, held in Moscow in June 1934, but Attila was not. In fact, he had been dropped from the official list of 'accepted writers'; and his work was publicaly rejected by the Party. Scandalous and absurd, the affair was as outrageous as it was dangerous and damaging. Attila's Hungarian comrades understood what Big Brother expected them to do; they withdrew from him. Once again, the young man lost his "family". The despair and disappointment he suffered only reinforced his sense of failure and exclusion; he felt burned, rejected, and humiliated by this experience.

And yet this turmoil notwithstanding, József went on to compose some of the most beautiful lyrics of his age. Among them emerges the 'Ode' (1933), with its slowly rolling, dreamy opening:

> I am alone on these glittering crags.
> A sinuous breeze
> floats delicious, the infant summer's
> suppertime simmer and ease.
> I school my heart into this silence.
> Not so arduous –
> All that is vanished is aswarm in me,
> my head is bowed, and my hand is
> vacuous.
>
> I see the mane of the mountain –
> each little leafvein
> leaps with the light of your brow.
> The path is quite deserted,
> I see how your skirt is floated
> in the wind's sough.
> Under the tender, the tenuous bough
> I see you shake out your hair, how it clings,
> your soft, trembling breasts; behold
> – just as the Szinva-stream glides beneath –
> the round white pebbles of your teeth,
> and how the welling laughter springs
> tumbling over them like fairy gold.

But this is only the prelude to the breathtaking peregrinations in the biological, intellectual, spiritual, and cosmological realms where the speaker takes his audience. Then, surging into a last breathtaking crescendo, he closes the journey:

> How high is this dawn-shadowy sky!
> Armies are glittering in its ore.
>
> Radiance anguishing to the eye.
> Now I am lost, I can no more.
> Up in the world I hear it batter,
> my heart's old roar.

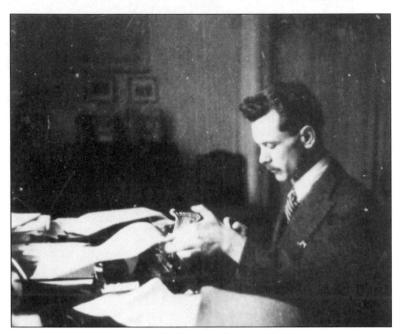

ABOVE: *Attila József, Budapest, early 30s.*
BELOW: *Attila József with Thomas Mann, 13 January 1937.*

Yet 'Ode' doesn't end outdoors, with the breathless dithyramb of the glitter of the sky's ore, rather, in the room of the lovers, with two simple, song-like four-liners playing out the scene:

> (Now the train's going down the track,
> maybe today it'll carry me back,
> maybe my hot face will cool down today,
> maybe you'll talk to me, maybe you'll say:
>
> Warm water's running, there's a bath by and by!
> Here is a towel, now get yourself dry!
> The meat's on the oven, and you will be fed!
> There where I lie, there is your bed.)

Despite his lyrical fecundity, the disintegration of his confidence in a political-ethical stance corroded József's self-image, his hope for a better future, and his trust in his friends and comrades. In fact, there was not much left on which he could build his trust. Studying the question of extremism and orthodoxy for awhile and arriving at a new understanding, he started to compare Soviet ideology to the doctrine of the Nazis. He spun out this idea in several later poems, among them in the extraordinarily beautiful lyrics for Thomas Mann, who came to Budapest in January 1937 for a reading of the Joseph tetralogy: [13]

> tell us the joy of beauty, and the pain,
> lifting our hearts from mourning to desire.
> We've laid poor Kosztolányi in the mire,
> and on mankind, as cancer did on him,
> horrible monster states gnaw limb by limb,
> and we, aghast, ask what's the next disease,
> whence fall new wolvish ideologies,
> what newer poison boils within our blood –
> how long, and where, you can still read aloud?

What is essential in this context is both József's formulation of the 'horrible monster states' that 'gnaw mankind' 'limb by limb' and his summary of the Nazi and Soviet doctrines as 'new wolvish ideologies'. They show his penetrating insight into the essential commonalities of these two dictatorships, an insight confined to just a very few on the Left in 1937. They also show his courage in dealing with changes affecting his own development. For József was now pressed to come to terms with his own self-definition as a 'proletarian poet', true to his roots, fighting against the inhumanity of the factory world, for the sake of what he held to be 'justice, spirit, and rationality', with the masses on his side. If he couldn't place the thrust in the Party, where could he? The myth he spun many years ago that had supported his personal ethos started to disintegrate as soon as the early 30s. Its splinters chafed against both his sense of selfhood and his relationship with Judit. Although she cared for him and tried to keep his life in order, the couple separated.

Attila became Dr Edit Gyömrői's patient during the year of 1934. And he fell in love with her so desperately and so intensely that neither she nor he could handle the affair. From here on, his fate took on an ever darkening edge.

She wasn't his first analyst, though. The young man had begun treatment with Sámuel Rapaport in 1931. Editing Rapaport's book on gastrointestinal manifestations of nervous disorders, Attila recognised his own real or imagined 'nervous symptoms'. Instead of paying Attila for his editorial help, Rapaport offered him psychoanalytic treatment and Attila trotted along faithfully. But the sessions didn't bring any change, not for a long time at any rate. Months went by, years even; yet he still continued to live with Judit, nursing the wounds of his past; he was still looking for a job and still involved in a major warfare with the Party. But then things got worse. The phantoms of his childhood started to dominate his daily life. His sense of failure undermined his balance. He felt exhausted: attacked, insulted and rejected. His poetry was read by only a small number of people; the Party had expelled him and his comrades had left him. At times, he sank into a deep depression. After years of treatment, Rapaport decided that what Attila needed was a new analyst. Some of his close friends recommended Gyömrői. With Bertalan Hatvany's offer to pay for the treatment, Gyömrői's sessions with him started in the autumn of 1934 (possibly early 1935); they went on until November 1936.

Whether or nor it was true that he could have been helped had his analysis been conducted more "appropriately" is a question we cannot decide; volumes of in-depth studies argue about the case. Nor can we measure the extent of the damage he suffered because of Gyömrői's treatment; this issue, too, has been abundantly investigated. What we must not fail to note, however, is that his passionate love for her intensified during the first few months of the treatment, and that as time went by, his emotions grew more and more out of control, more and more desparate, more and more frustrated. Some of his friends started to worry about his state of mind.

In his doctors' opinion, he was schizophrenic. Perhaps he was; but his poetic structures show no sign of disintegration, no sign of a mental breakdown.[14] Not once did his 'schizophrenia' manifest itself in a 'decomposition of verse construction' or in 'an increasingly meaningless jumble of words' which typically characterise, according to a number of experts, the work of poets suffering from this disorder.[15] As a matter of fact, even in his worst times, he created poems containing exacting logical patterns, ever new sounds and ever more intricate metre, always preserving a precarious formal balance between feeling and order. Also his lyrical ideas are glitteringly clear, at once personal and mythic. They just turn darker, more compulsive, more guilt-ridden. But still, amidst that darkness, they continue communicating a purity and a beauty of unspeakable tenderness:

> But now I know. This quivering truth discloses
> with its great light the primal crime, exposes
> its blackening corpse coffined within my heart.
>
> And if I did not speak, my mouth would mutter,
> would that you would bear a sin as bitter:
> I should not feel then so alone, apart.

Attila József, 1936.

And again and again, he invokes the ghosts harrying him; as the
song 'Sin' (August 1935) reveals:

> I killed, I'll tell them. Don't know whom.
> Perhaps my father might
> I watched his lifeblood stream and spume
> one dark and clotted night.

The poems of 1936 reveal his angst-ridden mind, even though his
verse shows more riches and formal exactness than ever before.
Many of them call on Gyömrői, demanding her unconditional
love, quite obviously, the love his mother never gave him, as 'You
Gave Me Childhood' (May 1936) does:

> Feed me – I hunger. Cover me – I shiver.
> Attend to me – I am a clumsy fool.
> Your absence blows through me, a draught's cold river.
> Command – and fear shall leave me, as you rule.

Gyömrői didn't know what to do. She was afraid of him. Engaged
to somebody else, she was reluctant to continue the sessions with
Attila. But she did so anyway. By the fall of 1936, the unfortunate
"affair" was well-known to a number of people, playing itself out
in the front of his friends and his family. Attila's temper running
short, he couldn't take the tension. In 'Agony' (November 1936),
he accused her publicly:

> Let her hear it:
> she denied her only merit;
> blithely, to a creature fleeing
>
> hither, thither,
> wandering it knows not whither,
> *grudged the last retreat of being.* [emphasis mine]

And as if this weren't enough, he composed 'Desolation' (November/
December 1936), lashing out at Edit with a ruthless ferocity, rarely
revealed in the lyrics of high art:

> May insects walk upon your eye. May greenish
> velvety mould befuzz your breasts. You flung
> me into desolation and I vanish.
> Grind up your teeth; devour your human tongue.

And it gets worse; his curses create more and more horror:

> Whom do you squeeze now? If you have a baby
> May his sole pleasure be to turn, and turn,
> You blinking at him, while about you, maybe,
> Full-gutted alligators flop and churn.
>
> Supine upon this bed I lie quite numbly,
> I see my eye: you look at me with it.
> Die! This I wish so brutishly, so dumbly,
> That I believe that I could die of it.

After the sessions stopped with Gyömrői, a new psychoanalyst arrived on the scene: Robert Bak.

In the meantime, Attila became editor of a new journal *Szép Szó* [The Luminous Word], a publication he started with his friend Ignotus. The journal's task was to counteract the growing power of the country's right wing by spreading a left-liberal point of view that emphasised the centrality of rational argument and humanism. With the Popular Front's decision to relax the tension between the Social Democrats and the Communists, the conflicts eased up among the various leftist groups, in every country. Attila wasn't alone anymore. Around him emerged a community of people that hadn't been there before. Some of them became contributors to the journal. But *The Luminous Word* wasn't restricted to essays alone. It carried several of József's own verses as well as the lyrics of other poets, including pieces by outstanding writers and essayists. In fact, professionally, Attila flourished in the last two years of his life; despite his deteriorating mental health and his unabating financial struggle, he composed some of his most striking, most beautiful poems during this period.

On 20 February 1937, Attila József met Flóra Kozmutza, a young psychologist, in the house of their mutual friends the Dániels. Flóra was interested in psychology in general and in the Rorschach Test in particular; so much so, that, in Németh's words, she 'chased after victims' whom she could involve in her study.[16] The Dániels provided her with such 'victims' by inviting a number of their friends, whom they introduced to Flóra. Right away, she tried out the Rorschach on Attila, stopping only when he got bored with it. He, in turn, recited several of his poems for the guests present at the Dániels that afternoon. He also fell in love with Flóra; perhaps more so than he had ever been in love before. This devotion is reflected in a string of love poems, that constitute a major part in József's lyrical output. What differentiates these poems from the rest? Is their particular world reaching outside the bounds of József's lyrics? It is. In fact, they combine the sweet purity of hymnals with the air, colours and feelings of the ancient bucolic tradition. They also echo the sonorities and metre of the past, reiterated and re-invented by a new love-drunk devotion. In 'Hexameters' (February 1937), the first one in this series, the persona celebrates his excitement in highly musical, image-laden lyrics:

> See then how much, how frighted-from-swoon I adore you, Flóra!
> Now in this chattering lovely meltworld the grief of my heart you
> dissolve, as a bandage is washed from a scar – and I tingle with quickening.

Listen: your name is a floodtide eternal, a delicate brightness,
a charm, and I shiver to think how I could have existed without you.

This mingling of exultant music, devotional praise and bucolic images is only crystallised in the last piece of the series, 'Be Measured!':

she, the dew upon the grasses,
truth, where a dubious shadow passes,
tramples my nightmare serpents' faces
Washes with smiles my sorrows' traces.

Simple water is amazing:
pure as water tastes her kissing;
she calls me home from bullies' chasing,
in her eyes a pony grazing.

And, then, with utmost grace and elegance, the ancient lineage reappears in full beauty, suffused by a deep devotion:

Hail to you, announced and treasured,
love me, always be remembered,
and, lest your praise be lost or beggared,
thus forever you are measured.

But there was a problem. József's poetic flourish notwithstanding, Flóra couldn't 'trample' Attila's 'nightmare serpents' faces'; nor could she 'call him home from bullies' chasing' for a simple reason: Flóra didn't love Attila. She was dazzled by his genius, enchanted by the poems he composed, and, probably, flattered by the intensity of Attila's adoration. But she didn't love him. And despite the fact that she went out with him frequently, especially in the first few months of their relationship, she was distant as well as careful to keep herself out of any romantic involvement. Thus, Attila, who asked her to marry him the day after their first meeting, and who became busy in building up this sandcastle of eternal love, eventually had to face up to the reality of his rejection. First Gyömrői, then Flóra. Wasn't this too much? More than he could bear? All of this only magnified the major characters of his childhood: his father, his mother, his abandonment, his early suffering. In the summer of 1937, it appeared that his mental state was rapidly deteriorating. Upon the advice of Dr Bak and Attila's closest friends Németh, Ignotus, and Bertalan Hatvany, he was taken to a sanatorium and kept there intermittently until November. He still composed magnificent poetry, despite shock treatments and heavy medication.

But the problem wasn't solved: what about his future? With Bertalan Hatvany paying the enormously expensive hospital bills, and with the uncertainty of the extent and duration of the illness itself, a solution had to be found, acceptable to everybody. And it was. Attila would go with his sisters and Etus's children to a town on the Lake Balaton, Balatonszárszó, where he would be cared for by his family and recuperate. This turned out to be a tragic decision. First of all, Attila was very close to some of his friends in Budapest and wasn't at all close to his sisters at this particular time. Second, his work on the journal was tied to his discussions and exchange of ideas with his friends who lived in the capital. Even though he had done very little work lately, leaving Budapest meant separating himself from the environment in which he could carry out his work. This must have have magnified his sense of uselessness and loneliness. Despair rattles the bars of the brilliant composition 'No Flowers, but a Spike' (November 1937):

> Your nakedness you always flaunted,
> tore off the scabs from wounds you vaunted,
> you're famous, if that's what you wanted.
> And have you done your time? You fool.
>
> Did you give love? Who would embrace you?
> Fugitive! who would even chase you?
> Just make the best of what will face you:
> no breadknife, and of course no bread.
>
> You're in the Seven Tower for good.[17]
> Be glad if you have firewood,
> glad for a pillow to your bed,
> be a good boy, lay down your head.

But in his last poem 'And So I've Found My Native Country' (24 November), pain and resignation combine with a transparent, other-worldly calm:

> …Spring, summer, autumn, all are lovely;
> but winter's loveliest for one
> who hopes for hearth and home and family
> only for others, when all's done.

Ten days later, on 3 December, he stood up before supper and announced that he was going out for a walk. Although they let him leave, his sisters started to worry almost immediately. But the children needed their supper. Etus finished cooking and dressed as fast as she could: she was going to run after him. But first, she had to put on her boots. About ten minutes had passed since he left. Just as she got ready, they heard someone crossing the yard. They calmed down, thinking he was back. But there was a knock. Fright overcame them, for that couldn't be him. Tearing the door open, they saw the village idiot standing there, sobbing. He tried to tell them what happened. Three children had seen Attila walking, then running towards the railway. They said he had slipped through the crossing-gate, bent down, and laid his hands on the rail. A goods train, standing still for a while, suddenly started moving. Knocking him over, it broke his neck. His body turned. Then his right arm was cut off. The train dragged him along for a stretch before it stopped.

As if hit by lightning, the literary circles of Hungary were jolted to the core; they started mourning. It took a few years before the nation did the same. Today's Hungary not only sees and hears and speaks in his vein, but it has also made his life and fate part of its own history, of its own ethos. And the beauty and creative energy of József's lyrics expand beyond the national borders: his poems move, charm, and amaze us in whatever language they resound.

NOTES:

1. Attila József has already been translated into English several times. His translators include: John Bátki, *Winter Night: Selected Poems of Attila József* (Budapest: Corvina and Oberlin College Press, 1997); John Bátki, trs, George Gömöri & James Atlas, eds, Attila József: *Selected Poems and Texts* (Cheadle: Carcanet Press, 1973); Péter Hargitai, *Perched on Nothing's Branch: Selected Poetry of Attila József* (Tallahassee: Apalachee Press, 3rd ed. 1993); Thomas Kabdebo, ed, *Attila József: Poems*, trs Michael Beavor & Michael Hamburger (London: Danubia Books, 1966); Edwin Morgan, *Fragments by Attila József* (Edinburgh: Morning Star Publications, 1992); Edwin Morgan, *Collected Translations* (Manchester: Carcanet Press, 1996); Lucas Myers, trs, 'Poems by Attila József' in *Periplus: Poetry in Transition* (New York: Oxford University Press, 1993); and Anton N. Nyerges, *Poems of Attila József*, Program in East European and Slavic Studies, 3 (Buffalo: Hungarian Cultural Foundation, 1973).
2. Hungarian and Bulgarian historical characters.
3. Áron József didn't go to the US, though, as was generally believed by his family, friends, and co-workers. Rather, he settled down in his native Romania and lived there for the rest of his life.
4. Attila József, *Szabad ötletek jegyzéke* [A Register of Free Associations] (Budapest: Atlantisz [Medvetánc], 1990), 28.
5. Andor Németh, *József Attiláról* [On Attila József] (Budapest: Gondolat, 1989), 435 (hereafter cited as AJ and page numbers).
6. Attila József, 'Az Istenek halnak, az Ember él' ['Gods Die; Man Lives'] *Toll* [The Pen] (10 January 1930), 14 (hereafter cited as 'Gods Die' and page numbers).
7. József, 'Gods Die', 23.
8. Lajos Hatvany, 'József Attiláról' ['On Attila József'], *Kritika* [Criticism], 8 (1977), 15.
9. Andor Németh, 'József Attila élete és kora' ['Attila József's Life and Age'], *Csillag* [Star], 4 (1948), 34.

10. Mihály Babits, *Irók a két háború között* [Writers in the Interwar Period] (Budapest: Nyugat, n.d.), 11.

11. It is one of the tragic ironies of life that he was nominated for the Prize in December 1937, and had he lived, he would have received it in 1938. e.g. Gábor Murányi, ed., *Napló és visszaemlékezés* [Diary and Remembrance], Judit Szántó (Budapest: Argumentum Kiadó, 1997), 208.

12. Németh, AJ, 90.

13. Thomas Mann planned to stay for four days in Budapest. But the permission the Horthy police gave the great writer allowed for a three-day stop only. See Antal Mádl & Judit Györi, eds, *Thomas Mann und Ungarn: Essays, Dokumente, Bibliographie* [Thomas Mann and Hungary: Essays, Documents and Bibliography] (Köln/Wien: Bohlau Verlag, 1977), 362. Dezsö Kosztolányi (1885-1936), one of the great Hungarian poets of the 20th century.

14. See on this question Antal Bókay, Ferenc Jádi & András Stark, *'Köztetek lettem én bolond...': Sors és vers József Attila utolsó éveiben* ['It's Among You that I Became Crazy': Fate and Poem in the Last Years of Attila József] (Budapest: Magvető Könyvkiadó, 1982), especially, 119-84.

15. Georg Klein, *Pietà*, trs, Theodore & Ingrid Friedmann (Cambridge/London: MIT Press, 1992), 71.

16. Németh, AJ, 299.

17. After the armies of Sultan Suleyman occupied the Hungarian capital in 1541, they kidnapped Balint Török, a nobleman and protector of the infant King John II. Török died in Istanbul. In one of Hungary's most popular youth novels, *The Stars of Eger* by Géza Gárdonyi, the tragic fate of Török is part of the main plot. The book portrays his capture, his cruel imprisonment in the sultan's fortress named the 'Seven Tower' and his death after many years of agony, forever separated from his beloved wife and two children. The image of the Seven Tower evokes in the Hungarian reader a sense of betrayal, utter loss, homelessness and isolation.

ATTILA JÓZSEF, 1929

THE *ARS POETICA* OF ATTILA JÓZSEF

Frederick Turner

When Attila József came to the edge of the world, as he did every time he sat down to write a poem, he saw all of reality laid out beneath him like a landscape, its coasts and fields and rivers, its wide sandy reaches, its bright green marshes. He rises like a shaman on his visionary flight into the sky; past and future, and the forces of the present that transform the latter into the former, are prophetically clear to him.

> Eagle, gigantic, diving
> heaven's echoey precipices!
> What winged thing's this, arriving
> from voids and nothingnesses!
>
> ('Eagle')

> the dawns commissioned in their sky-fought wars,
> the leaping suns and finely trembling stars,
> around my quiet and sleepy head are hurled,
> my temperature's the glowing of the world –
>
> ('Medallions')

At the heart of his vision is a majestic cosmology, and his most central work as a poet is to reveal it in words.

> In heaven's iron-blue vault revolves
> a cool and lacquered dynamo.
> The word sparks in my teeth, resolves
> – oh, noiseless constellations! – so –
>
> ('Beyond Hope')

Attila József's work was ended by his suicide. He thus did not have the chance to lay out his cosmological vision in a systematic way where its philosophical importance can be seen for what it is – rather than as merely the mysterious and impressive metaphors used by a poet to decorate his observations and apostrophes. The last service of the translator is therefore to show the elegant logic, the scientific insight, and the formidably coherent organisation of his philosophical system. What was it he saw from that place of the halted breath, of fine and brilliant crystalline light? József's cosmology can be divided into five major elements:

> The universe of existent being.
> The great void that lies beyond the edge or shore or rupture that bounds the universe.

The forces of collective human creativity and love that continue nature's own work of pushing out the boundaries of being into the future.
The conscious self of the poet.
The world-creating activity of poetry.

The Existent World

For József, the universe as it is is ordered, coherent, interdependent, and maintained through the dialectical tension of its elements. It has a necessity which is both beautiful and fateful. The image he uses is a homely one from a craft he must obviously have had to practise often: chopping and stacking wood. A well-stacked cord of firewood holds together and holds up, paradoxically, by the tendency of all of its components to fall apart and down:

> Just like split firewood stacked together,
> the universe embraces all,
> so that each object holds the other
> confined by pressures mutual,
> all things ordained, reciprocal.

> ('Consciousness')

These lines first appear in '(Self-devouring...)', his moving apology to Mihály Babits, the elder poet he had previously lampooned in his cruel poem 'On a Poet'. There they serve as a demonstration to his distinguished former enemy of the seriousness of his philosophical views, and as an exposition of the way in which two poets of opposed tendencies, the flautist (Babits) and the piper (himself) might cooperate in a universal harmony. Like Pindar, József associates the harmony of music with the skill of joinery, which so arranges the joints of posts and beams in a roof, that storms make the bond tighter. The lines were obviously important to him, for he repeats them verbatim in 'Consciousness', one of his most important philosophical poems, and elaborates them into an ontology.

If one were to characterise József's ontology in formal philosophical terms, one might call him a realist. But his differs from all the traditional brands of realism. He is not a commonsense realist, who accepts the world as it seems. He finds a higher and deeper reality in things than the illusions of habit, custom, appetite, opinion and fashion:

> Those other poets – why should I worry
> how they defile their paunch and crop?

With gin and trumped-up imagery
let them feign drunkenness, throw up.

I leap the time's saloon, its liquor,
strive for intelligence, and beyond!
My brain is free, I'll not play sucker
and serve their fatuous demi-monde.

Let nature be your test and measure!
Let yourself eat, drink, sleep, embrace!
No pain shall make me serve the pleasure
of powers so crippling, vile and base.

('Ars Poetica')

He is not a transcendental Platonic or Christian realist either, for
he sees that deeper reality as immanent, indwelling in the physical
immediacy of the world rather than suspended above it in a limbo
of perfection, and as dynamic and evolving rather than fixed for-
ever in an eternal present.

Time oozes down, and I no longer
suck the breast milk of fairytales;
I quaff the real world in my hunger,
whose foamy head is heaven's pales.

('Ars Poetica')

For József, reality is a river, like the Danube with its cargo of melon-
rinds and pepper-parings like moons, and apples like planets. Its
ideal forms are not static and eternal geometries outside it, but
more like the pillars of fire and smoke in the book of Exodus that
go on before us within the real world, leading us into the future,
transforming themselves according to the conditions of the time.

But József is not a phenomenological realist either. He does not
succumb to the great temptation of artists and continental philo-
sophers of our century, to escape the drudgery of scientific know-
ledge by dismissing it as secondary to immediate sensory experience.
József's scientific knowledge is astonishingly accurate; as a student
he evidently paid much more attention to the sciences than is usual
for poets since the Romantic period. He knows that nature con-
structs itself, and our constructions of it are only a part of nature's
own continuous self-articulation. He knows that how we understand
something intellectually can deepen and transform our experience
of it, especially if that understanding has the surprise of genuine
scientific fact. The experience of nature provides us with our intel-
ligence. Nature teaches us not just in the Romantic sense, by the
subjective just-so stories that tell us about the consequences of moral
action, but as revealed by scientific research and instrumentation

and perceived by an *informed* imagination on fire with love for the way things actually are in themselves. Our human experience does not transcend nature, but shares in nature's own self-transcendence as the species that nature evolved to know itself.

József schools his extraordinary sensorium into an experience that is both phenomenologically immediate and scientifically true. For instance, his understanding of genetics and cytology in the following passage is quite uncanny:

> My mother was a Kún, my father Magyar
> in part, perhaps Romanian in full.
> My mother's mouth gave me the sweetest nectar,
> my father's mouth, the truth as beautiful.
> If I but stir, they do embrace each other.
> It grieves me sometimes when I think of how
> time flies, decays. Such matter is my mother.
> 'You see when we are not!...' they tell me now.
>
> They speak to me, my being's patrimony,
> in this my weakness, thus I may be well,
> recalling that I'm greater than the many,
> each of my ancestors in every cell –
> I am the Ancestor, in my division
> I multiply, blithely turn dam and sire,
> and they achieve their double parturition,
> many times many making one self fire!
>
> ('By the Danube')

Nature is our own heredity; the past is alive in us, in our genes, our cells, our muscles: the moment when our parental sperm and egg came together is recapitulated in every present moment as our cells divide in the process of metabolism. József's clear understanding of the physical reality of the world, even our own bodies, can be unsettling until we accept its beauty. He has no illusions about what is going on in his beloved's body; she is a physical world in herself, populated by her own society of living organisms:

> Your capillaries, like a blood-red rose,
> ceaselessly stir and dance.
> There that eternal current seethes and flows
> and flowers as love upon your countenance,
> to bless with fruit your womb's dark excellence.
> A myriad rootlets broider round
> and round your stomach's tender ground,
> whose subtle threadings, woven and unwound,
> unknit the very knot whereby they're bound,
> that thus thy lymphy cell-brood might abound,
> and the great, leaved boughs of thy lungs resound
> their whispered glory round!

The *eterna materia* goes marching on
happily through your gut's dark cavern-cells,
and to the dead waste rich life is given
within the ardent kidneys' boiling wells!

Billowing, your hills arise, arise,
constellations tremble in your skies,
lakes, factories work on by day and night,
a million creatures bustle with delight,
millipede,
seaweed,
a heartless mercy, gentle cruelty,
your hot sun shines, your darkling north light broods,
in you there stir the unscanned moods
of a blind incalculable eternity.

('Ode')

There is, however, nothing reductionist or materialist in József's realism either. After all, he was thrown out of the Communist Party partly perhaps for his reactionary love of traditional poetic forms and metres, as well as for the heterodoxy of his views. The spiritual and the imaginative are for him just as substantial a part of the world as are matter and energy – indeed, more so, because they are more immediately active and represent a further refinement of nature's evolutionary process.

But nature also is the past, and since its reality as past cannot be undone, it stands before us as law rather than choice. It is awesome, beautiful; it is our teacher; it is our heredity and patrimony. But it also gives us our drives and needs and desires, our hunger for food, sex, shelter, progeny, rest, comfort. It expresses itself in the laws of historical necessity, of technological momentum, economic inertia, the social system we are born into. The existent universe, as expressed in the constraints of history, is a prison:

And now I stand, and through the sky-dome
the stars, the Dippers, shine and burn,
like bars, the sign of jail and thraldom,
above a silent cell of stone.

('Consciousness')

In his dark and sinister poem 'Tiszazug', about a peasant village where a series of horrible crimes had been committed, József gives us a picture of the limitations of nature:

The hen clucks sadly in its roost
under the gutter's sheltered lee,
as if she were the old hag's ghost
that haunts the place beseechingly.

Indoors more freckled livestock lurk,
bluish old loonies, addledly,
who grunt aloud at times, and jerk,
to stop the flow of revery.

Because indeed there's much to brood
when there's no hoeing to be done.
The sweet soft gossip-pipes are chewed,
a thread in broken fingers spun.

For what's an old one worth? He drops
his spoon, he drools, is fed; so frail
that if he serves the piglets' slops
they knock him down and spill the pail.

And soft's the homestead, warm the pen.
The nightfall dangles from a star!
Hard is the firmament. A wren
limps peeping in a pine-bough's scar.

('Tiszazug')

It is natural for humans to rise above the rest of nature, and un-
natural when they do not. Mere natural happiness, in 'Consciousness',
is a fat pig in its swill:

I've seen what they call happiness:
soft, blonde, it weighed two hundred kilos;
it waddled smiling on the grass,
its tail a curl between two pillows.
Its lukewarm puddle glowed with yellows,
it blinked and grunted at me – yes,
I still remember where it wallows,
touched by the dawns of blissfulness.

('Consciousness')

The fear and conservatism engendered by a life limited to natural
drives is what puts the common man and woman at the mercy of
the rich and powerful, who can play upon their weakness and thus
gain their support against progress. If there is nothing beyond the
realm of existent being, we are trapped within its laws. But for
József there is indeed something beyond being: nothingness itself.

'Frost's Glittering Axe-head'

Who would this poem's reader be,
must know its poet, must love me,
sailing upon the vacuum,
knowing, as seers do, what's to come...

('Who would this poem')

The poet comes to the edge or shore of the world. Beyond it there is nothing, a clean and glittering void, as untrodden as the very snow that will fall tomorrow, but not at 180 degrees to the line of the past, as the quotidian future is, but rather, so to speak, at 90 degrees. Sometimes he will set sail in that mysterious void. He comes to that place in ecstasy, extreme despair, exhaustion, at the end of his tether, in a contemplative trance, in the violent exhilaration of sexual joy. Often there is a strange flash of light and a soft whicker, like the sound and glitter of a blade, or a bolt of lightning before the thunder; the experience of instantaneity combined with a preternatural stillness.

Slowly, musingly

I am as one who comes to rest
by that sad, sandy, sodden shore
and looks around, and undistressed
nods his wise head, and hopes no more.

Just so I try to turn my gaze
with no deceptions, carelessly.
A silver axe-swish lightly plays
on the white leaf of the poplar tree.

Upon a branch of nothingness
my heart sits trembling voicelessly,
and watching, watching, numberless,
the mild stars gather round to see.

('Beyond Hope')

This place of emptiness and void is also the place that calls existent reality into being. Nothingness condenses into a world: József here anticipates the insights of quantum cosmology, which regards vacuum as an inherently unstable state which must generate fluctuations at some critical level of microcosmic indeterminacy, fluctuations that can balloon up into a physical universe. Aristotle's dictum, *ex nihilo nihil fit*, out of nothing nothing can be made, is as wrong for the quantum cosmologists and for József as it is for the book of Genesis. Here is one of József's uncanny anticipations of the quantum vacuum and the evolution of the initial singularity into a cosmos:

Nothingness so flits within it
as a something's dust, a minute
past its prime...

Nothingness so flits and dances
as if it a something were;
universe expands, condenses
to the future, floating there;
space, the sea, the branched tree-branches,

dogs whose howling avalanches,
sing its sphere...

I, my chair, each fry and phylum,
and the Earth beneath the Sun,
solar system, this asylum,
with the galaxies strive on –

('On Our Poet and His Time')

The experience of this place on the edge of everything touches off
in him a wild beauty of poetic metaphor:

As fairy-glittering as thought, as bright,
twinkles the winter night.

Darkness' silver silence locks
the moon onto the Earth's still parallax.

A black crow flies across the frostcold sky;
silence cools in my mouth. Bone, do you hear it?
Molecules tinkle, crystals ramify.

In what glass case or cabinet
glitter such winter nights?

('Winter Night')

A few lines later in this poem he uses the metaphor we have looked
at in 'Consciousness,' of the well-stacked cord of wood, to describe
the *chora* or self-constituted container of the universe, glimpsed
by metaphor in the cloud of sparks thrown up by a locomotive:

Across the plain,
like its own small winter night,
a freight train sets its plume of smoke alight,
chora to contain
in a cord's bourne, infinite,
the turning, burning, dying stars' domain.

('Winter Night')

Nothingness, then, is the dynamic incompleteness that draws the
universe on into new creation. But in his more despairing mode
he recognises that nothingness as his very own self; he is a hole in
being, his poem only the bright corolla of radiation that is emitted
as the matter of his experience plunges past the event-horizon of
his engulfing emptiness.

Think: I have nothing left to give away,
no one to have and hold. What I called 'me'
is nothing too. I gnaw its crumbs today,

and when this poem is done it will not be...
As space is by a searchlight, I am pierced through
by naked sight:

('My Eyes Jump In and Out...')

And in this place József encounters a gigantic and terrifying ghost: God Himself, the Ancient of Days, the absent father whose corpse still feels full of the power to punish.

> but I scream in vain endeavour:
> love me: I'll be good, I shiver
> in the terror of His frown.
>
> ('The Scream')

As Nietzsche knew, even the absence or death of God leaves in the language and the world an enormous and unnavigable God-shaped hole. Like Melville's Captain Ahab, József attempts to strike through the mask, to challenge this authority that has forever preempted the poet's power to create, the people's own self-evolution:

> I'd choke my very breath, to die,
> your rod and staff thus disobeying,
> and look you boldly in the eye,
> you empty, human-faced unbeing!
>
> ('Tumble out of the Flood')

That palpable absence demands of us an inhuman perfection, a renunciation of physicality that can tempt us toward suicide, and that can freeze up the loving sensuality of life:

> O bony chastity of heaven –
> starved hoarfrost of a feast ungiven!
> Unwinking, impeturbable!
> Trusting that I'll do what is noble!
>
> I live on diamond-chilly herring,
> etheric furniture my dwelling,
> my nails grow sharp and curve and harden,
> their roses whiten in their garden.
>
> ('Rime')

Yet at other times József recognises the sweetness and the loving-ness of the divine as it makes its presence felt in human history, calling us prophetically toward a world of human fulfilment. Perhaps his most charming and delightful poem celebrates with the swarthy Magi the birth of Christ:

> In excelsis, Lord of Hosts, Lord of Hosts!
> We are not some dry old priests.
>   What we heard was at your borning,
>   kingdom of the poor was dawning.
>   We looked in for just a glimmer,
>   heavenly king and our redeemer!
>   Caspar's what my name would be,
>   sort of earthly king, you see.
>
> ('The Kings of Bethlehem')

József's ambivalence about the fellow-occupant of that creative void is fundamental:

> Terrify me, my hidden God,
> I need your wrath, your scourge, your thunder;
> quick, come tumble out of the flood,
> lest nothingness sweep us asunder.

('Tumble out of the Flood')

Human Creativity and Love: the Evolutionary Dynamo

Between the beautiful and ineluctable order of the past and the chilly perfection of the empty *potentia* József finds the vital forces of human creativity. In one sense they are the continuation of the dynamic dialectic of nature itself; in another sense they are nature's own transcendence of herself into a new kind of freedom, which because it is conscious of itself is uniquely self-determining. Today we would have different words for that dialectical process: we might call it chaotic emergence, bifurcation at the point of critical complexity, self-organisation in far-from equilibrium conditions, the tracing out of a strange attractor by a nonlinear dynamical system. József intuits the process as the turbulence of a river, especially the Danube, and imagines the emergence of new natural and historical forms as the inundation of its banks. Life floods over the very boundaries it has set for itself:

> Because the cosmos is a bonus,
> gives more than is its due or onus,
> life overflows death's final shore,
> whelms the heart's margins in its roar...

('To Flóra')

He even seems to see in the sky the fractal attractor of the process, like a rich fabric in the process of its making and unmaking:

> I stared from underneath the evening
> into the cogwheel of the sky –
> the loom of all the past was weaving
> law from those glimmery threads, and I
> looked up again into the sky
> from underneath the steams of dreaming
> and saw that always, by and by,
> the weft of law is torn, unseaming.

('Consciousness')

Collectively, those vital forces of human creativity, that tear the old law apart to make room for new, act through the masses, nations,

52

the world-spirit itself. The pressure of human technological and scientific progress creates the machinery that sets us free from drudgery, ignorance, fear and early death. More and more of nature submits to human will; but since human will is itself nature's own most creative and mysterious voice, nothing is lost thereby. There is in József none of that nostalgia for forgetfulness, the mysticism of blood and soil that hated technology, cosmopolitanism, conscious intention and economic productivity, the *völkisch* yearning for a pretechnological world of unmediated Being that was as strong in Hungary as in Dostoyevsky's Russia or Heidegger's Germany. He sees the danger of these views as clearly as did his admired Thomas Mann. József has no trace of the widespread antisemitism of the time. He is enthusiastic about clean schools, rural electrification, industrial efficiency and economic progress, and knowing at first hand what Marx called 'rural idiocy,' the short, brutal and greasy life of the peasant that has stunted human existence since the Neolithic, he has no illusions about the idyllic world of the Volk. Though the present economic system is its own kind of prison, controlled still by the dead hand of the old property-owners, and though its present inefficiency makes it a polluting menace to the rest of nature, it holds in a dialectical sense the potential for a new kind of society and a new natural/human world.

> Not God, nor even thoughts, but coal
> and oil and iron instead,
>
> the real material, created us
> and poured us, fiery-found,
> into the iron moulds of society,
> the ghoul that holds us bound,
> that we might be the conscience of the human
> on the eternal ground.
>
> After the priests, the warriors and the burghers,
> thus we became the true,
> the ultimate, observer of the laws;
> all man makes that is new,
> creation's essence, therefore thrums in us,
> as deep violas do.
>
> ('On the Edge of the City')

In another, more basic way, the force of human creativity expresses itself through human sexuality and the urge to have offspring. Collective production is founded upon and in turn supports individual reproduction.

> O you machines, birds, tree-branches, constellations!
> Our barren mother cries out for a child.
>
> ('No Shriek of Mine')

József yearned for a wife, for a family, for the simple pleasures of an evening meal surrounded by people he loved and who loved him. His wild and pathetic longings for sexual union with the women he fell in love with are not so much a matter of sensual desire as of a need for family, for the opportunity to give his life to a wife and children.

> For we'll beget a girl so pretty,
> clever and good; a brave wise boy;
> they'll save a shred of us, our pity,
> like sunfire from the Milky Way, –
> and when the Sun is guttering,
> our princelings in their sweet machines
> shall fly, and fearless, chattering,
> find stars to plow the earthly genes.
>
> ('March')

Thus both on the collective level and on the individual level, the urge to new creation drives the emergence of a future liberated from the constraints of the past. The economic impulse toward production and the sexual impulse toward reproduction are at their base the same thing: they are the source of joy.

> Lift up your heart,
> set fire to heaven's domains!
>
> Till it lights up our lovely sense of order,
> that urge to shapeliness
> by which the brain knows and acknowledges
> finite unboundedness:
> the outward forces of production and the inward
> instinctive drive to bliss...
>
> ('On the Edge of the City')

But József was never able to enjoy the riches of either production or reproduction: he died poor and childless. Heartbreakingly, these were the first and last words of poetry he wrote:

> I would like a lot of money:
> I'd eat roasted goose and honey,
> Cut the figure of a dandy,
> Buy the fifty-dollar candy.
>
> As I sucked my fancy candy,
> I would brag from May to Monday,
> In my fine clothes and my villa,
> Just how well life treats Attila.
>
> ('Dear Joco' – c. 1916; he was about 11 years old)

> Spring, summer, autumn, all are lovely;
> but winter's loveliest for one

who hopes for hearth and home and family
only for others, when all's done.

('And So I've Found my Native Country'
– 24 November 1937, nine days before his death)

For József, the creative human power comes to its apex in the work of the poet. The poet hears and articulates the inchoate voice of the people as a whole, and shows to itself the process of production and liberation that animates nature and the human economy alike. This is from his grand and heroic poem on Ady, the Hungarian revolutionary poet:

> Magyar on Magyar soil, poet within it,
> he grasps in angry fists two clods of earth,
> above his breast the cloud rears infinite:
> but still his revolutions come to birth.
>
> He works on, unforgetting, unassuaging,
> there in the strange dark dwellings of the ground,
> a thousand acres thunder with his raging,
> he hunts the steppes, drives the winds round and round –
>
> ('In Memory of Ady')

The poet, then, combines in his work the inventive ingenuity of the maker, the technologist, with the organic, loving and nurturing role of the mother and father of a child. The force that is unleashed from the combination is creatively revolutionary, and when it encounters the fences and walls of tyranny, it can be violent. But its goal is harmony. The poet is to the half-conscious striving of humanity toward liberation, what humanity itself is to nature's unconscious struggle toward self-articulation.

> The poet – the word may rattle on his lips,
> but he (the engineer
> who serves the magic of the given world),
> seeing the future clear,
> as you without, so he within – constructs
> a new harmonic sphere.
>
> ('On the Edge of the City')

The Self

The self, for József, is a miraculous reflexive part of nature, the instrument by which nature comes to know itself. It is, indeed, based on primal animal needs that must be met, or else the self will starve, become warped, melt down, or turn toward its self-destruction.

My grapes, my purple clustering,
turn now to pea-pods festering.
Their tiny black eyes twirl and prickle,
    mixed with my tears they fall and trickle.

('Rime')

But when the self is healthy it is more than a function of society
or an economic unit: it is the leading edge of social change, the
only place where true progress can begin. The poet in particular
is charged with the construction, upon the base of nature and his-
tory, of a more humane world. But to do this the poet must first
construct, or reconstruct, his own self.

In 'Medallions' József gives us, in wild surrealist imagery, perhaps
the most profound account in literature of this terrifying, heroic
and magical activity. He harks back to his childhood, when he had
been sent into foster care with a peasant family without culture or
true compassion, who gave him a different name than his own and
put him to work as a swineherd. Here, instead of allowing his
deprivation and yearning for home to destroy him, as some children
might, he transformed his loss into what he calls 'medallions',
magical talismans or mandalas in which what is precious in the
self can be preserved. Many children collect curious and pretty
pebbles and watch with fascination the clottings of foam as they
twirl in their cocoa. But for the child Attila they are spells or runes
by which the self is simultaneously represented, hidden from harm,
buried and preserved. They are the child's self – that miraculous
clotting or turbulence about a point-attractor of absence that cre-
ates a centric order from which the world can be seen and known.
By means of these objectifications his inner person is given the
power to resurrect itself from the dead, bring back the lost moth-
er's breast, and metamorphose reality.

The images tumble out of him in amazing profusion: the
rounded chunk of banded quartz, the green stag-beetle, the dew-
drop, the jasper pebble shaped like a little pig or knuckle-bone,
the fresh cowpat, the apple with a worm in it, the frozen apple-
blossom, the spiral of foam on warm milk, the cold knife, the
loose button, the galaxies, the green lizard, the roundel of scum-
my suds in the serving-maid's pail (his mother's), a scrap of
stamped iron filigree, a fly in amber that looks like a thin little
attorney in tails, a heron's feather, his own little boy-penis, a
braided beard, cantaloupes like medieval crowns, and the faces of
people of all races, black, red, yellow and white. He even leaves a
stanza blank at the end, for each of us perhaps to add our own
medallions, our own moment when the medallion transforms from

private symbol of the psyche to universal archetype.

No life could be as tragic and needy as József's, and indeed he must have been difficult to get along with, especially for the women with whom he fell in love. But there is a noble and magnanimous mind fastened to that pitiful life; he went on trying to serve a people and a language that had not given him the things he had needed to be a complete human being. He emptied himself again and again in poetry; and sometimes, depleted, insane, in despair, he begins to curse his analyst.

> May insects walk upon your eye. May greenish
> velvety mould befuzz your breasts. You flung
> me into desolation and I vanish.
> Grind up your teeth; devour your human tongue.

> ('Desolation')

But even when he imagines his body as undergoing decay and death he leaves behind a mysterious residue of poetry:

> in death, my beard of hundredweights grows yet –

> And if my skin still twitches, heavens above,
> it's all that trickles through from spine to nave,
> the little fatties in their glowing swarms,
> the stars and galaxies, the small white worms –

> ('Medallions')

József achieved his learned and lofty metaphysics – one might almost call it a humane religion – in the teeth of appalling and cruel handicaps. They include his psychologically deprived and scarring childhood, together with literal hunger and malnutrition; an education cut short by prejudice and malice; the temptation of cheap Marxist explanations, and the pain of rejection by a party to which he had dedicated himself; the destructive effects of an evidently mismanaged Freudian psychoanalysis, by an analyst unable to handle her counter-transference; József's very powers of insight, that enabled him to know his own damage with terrible intimacy; his imaginative capacities for self-suggestion, that could, misguided by his therapists, cause him to dwell obsessively upon memories of cruel mistreatment; his dysfunctional sexual relationships, in which he sought a mother for a wife; his ruthless honesty and self-criticism; his courageous but foolhardy inability to resist a challenge, even when the challenge was to tinker with his own innermost mechanism; the threat of God as the authority of Being; and the incomprehension of many of his contemporaries, with the possible exception of Babits, whom he had insulted and antagonised.

This last handicap, of incomprehension by his public, is especially cruel; for I believe József to be an early victim of that ancient unconscious strategy for dealing with poets which has become so much a part of modernist cultural pathology. It is all right for a poet to be a self-destructive and pathetic monster, a victim, as long as he is not a teacher. The poet's role is to experience extreme emotional states in place of the ordinary person, preferably states which lead to sexual adventures and disasters, and to early death, suicide being the most poetic way to go. We have seen this syndrome in the lives of Dylan Thomas, Sylvia Plath, John Berryman and many others whose suicides had cheering sections. The poet is used as sacrificial scapegoat, as the gold standard that backs the moral currency of existentialist impulsiveness, as the assurance that grandeur of mind and spirit and imagination are paid for by misery and early death − so that we can prudently ignore the new view of the cosmos the poet presents, and are absolved of the onus to comprehend it in ourselves and live out its challenging implications. Some of his more sympathetic audience, like his mentor, the orientalist scholar Bertalan Hatvany, thought József would have been better off without his dangerous metaphysics, especially in the the summer of 1937, when József's mental condition was clearly deteriorating:

Space is my soul. And to its mother,
that great Space, it fain would fly.
Balloon to gondola, I tether
soul to body, to make I.
As neurotic sublimation
this my truth, or dream and vision,
they deny...

Come, my friend, let's face existence.
You must work here on the ground.
Empathy's become resistance.
Your wild fables are unsound.
Leave the former, leave the latter,
watch the twilight colours scatter,
melting round...

('On Our Poet and His Time')

In his poem 'For my Birthday' József claimed to be a teacher of his nation, and we only read him rightly if we take his claim seriously. Oddly enough, that Antal Horger who expelled József from school for being the author of this poem recognised something about the intellectual role of the poet that many admirers of the self-destructive artist do not. Part of the tragedy is that his Communist 'comrades' understood his threat to the agreed game of power as well as the conservative Horger did, and reacted the same way.

Poetry

For József the poet was an avatar of the ancient shaman-bard: a healer, a psychopomp, an explorer of new knowledge, the community's instrument of consciousness for apprehending its own dark realms of the spirit. He expresses what Shakespeare called 'the prophetic soul/ Of the wide world dreaming on things to come'. The poet is the trailblazer who marks the paths by which the historical and natural community can break its bonds and seek out wider freedoms and creative possibilities.

> His body is the soil's. His soul the digger's,
> whose hoe beats sometimes with a deep refrain.
> His grave's the freehold of three million beggars,
> where they may build, and plant, and reap the grain.
> His verse is law; and to the drum of Ady
> the hurled stones strike, the castle windows rend, –
> the plough cuts one more furrow in his body
> whose life will flower forever without end.

('In Memory of Ady')

The poet must therefore use the ancient shamanic devices of the drum and the pipe, which, like the lyre of Orpheus, are symbols of metrical form. Together with Radnóti and Babits, who resisted the new fashion of modernist free verse, József is a virtuoso of poetic metre and formal invention. His aware-ness of the need for formal control is explicit at the beginning of his magnificent 'Winter Night' – a poem composed in a very loose dithyrambic form, bridled only by rhyme and a consistent foot – where he exhorts himself: 'Discipline, discipline!' József's metrical traditionalism was perhaps another reason why his leftist contemporaries were as suspicious of him as were those on the conservative right. He indeed marched to a different, and much more ancient, drummer than did either.

In translating József's poems with Zsuzsanna Ozsváth, some of the greatest miracles occurred when I heard in Zsuzsi's voice the authentic cadence of the Finno–Ugric Altaic shaman. József's songs, some of which are virtually nonsense verse if one tries to make strict rational sense of them, would have been untranslatable without the ecstatic beat of his metrical drum and the shriek of his almost Japanese pipe. It is in these poems that we hear his metaphysics most purely of all, for it is here that the language is molten, white-hot, like the scarlet babe of liquid iron that the foundryman pours out in 'Night in the Outskirts'. His more discursive poems give us language that has cooled and hardened enough, by his blowing on it, for us to taste it with our logical faculties; but in such poems as

'The Last of Seven', 'Sitting, Standing, Killing, Dying', 'Chant', 'Medallions' and 'Beads', the words are still too hot.

> Mortal dweller, may your mother
> bear you seven times together!
> Once within a house that's burning,
> once in floods, the icefloes churning,
> once in bedlam, yelling, yearning,
> once in a wheatfield's soft turning,
> once in cloisters bell-intoning,
> once stied with pigs in grunts and groaning.
> What though these six cry out to heaven?
> You shall be the last of seven!
>
> ('The Last of Seven')

This poem is composed in the old Magyar trochaic tetrameter, the 'ancient eight,' the same metre as that of the magical Kalevala of the Finns (which József knew well). The meter survives the millennia of separation between the two related tribes far better than words themselves. We hear the same rhythm here, a primal celebration of living experience itself:

> or just sit in silent numbers,
> or burn Budapest to embers,
> feed a bird with crumbs and butter,
> hurl my stale bread to the gutter,
> leave my loving sweetheart weeping,
> grab her younger sister, groping,
> and, if world is my accounting,
> leave it, owing, unrelenting –
>
> ah, you binding and dissolving,
> you whose poem this is, evolving,
> you, my laughing and my crying,
> life, my choosing unto dying!
>
> ('Sitting, Standing, Killing, Dying')

In 'Chant', the metre is a trochaic version of the old tetrameter-trimeter drum-dance rhythm of the English ballad, which also underlies the most archaic Greek and Roman poetic rhythms: $/-/-/-/$; $/-/-/$. The old-fashioned and almost unintelligible peasant words of the song combine with the metre to cast us back to our common Nostratic-speaking ancestors, farming the plains and mountains of Asia and Europe:

> Once I milked a soot-nosed bull,
>   foxtale, hide and seek,
> in bull's milk my fate to tell,
>   foxtale, hide and seek.

In my seven pails' good steel,
   foxtale, hide and seek,
milkfoam gan to flame and flail,
   foxtale, hide and seek.
So to hide my flaming pail,
   foxtale, hide and seek,
plucked I roses pink and pale,
   foxtale, hide and seek.
People's rye rocks in the rose,
   foxtale, hide and fell,
bailiff's heart in cabbage-rows,
   foxtale, hide and fell.

     ('Chant')

And in 'Beads,' in the agony of frustrated sexual desire, József finds the same rhythm pumping:

Beads around your neck aglow,
Frogheads in the lake below.
Lambkin droppings,
Lambkin droppings in the snow.

     ('Beads')

The poet, for József, uses our instinctive drive toward beauty, which is both a continuation and recognition of the universe's own attraction toward self-organisation, as a guide. He thus unites nature with history in his own significant personal experience, by means of the contemplative discipline of poetic composition. He discovers the ur-language that lies beneath all natural tongues, that is fully translatable across cultures, and that is the warrant of our brotherhood and sisterhood as human beings. And he articulates the world-spirit through a measured song, which, as in a dream, combines the archetypal past with the experiential present, and ancient public symbols with new private ones.

ATTILA JÓZSEF, 1935

THE IRON-BLUE VAULT

Dear Jocó!

Stanza 1st
I would like a lot of money:
I'd eat roasted goose and honey,
Cut the figure of a dandy,
Buy the fifty-dollar candy.

Stanza 2
As I sucked my fancy candy,
I would brag from May to Monday,
In my fine clothes and my villa,
Just how well life treats Attila.

[1916-17 (?)]

Eleven or twelve years old when he wrote this poem, the boy called his older
sister 'Jocó' (pronounced 'Yotzo'). The stanza titling is his own.

Earth to Earth

Come, sister, for the sun our father, fleeing,
has trudged off to the village of far space.

Up there they've lit the moon's bright pane of being,
its hazed rose-window blooms with heavenly grace.

A hundred zigzag swallows now are rocking
in their nests, like your drunk words in my heart.

The tiny leaves are – like our fingers – shaking;
one earth-clod clasps another, not to part.

We too are scraps of earth, pressed close within it,
the tender herbage loves us, root and foil.

Love, let your body fall into my spirit,
we are the hidden furrow of the soil.

The night's dark lamb plods deeper into shadow,
its golden fleece is turned to black silk now.

And your blonde hair, as if it were a meadow,
filled full with the moon's opalescent glow.

[August 1923/1934]

No Shriek of Mine

No shriek of mine, it is the earth that thunders.
Beware, beware, Satan has gone insane;
Cling to the clean dim floors of the translucent springs,
Melt yourself to the plate glass,
Hide behind the diamond's glittering,
Beneath the stones, the beetle's twittering,
O sink yourself within the smell of fresh-baked bread,
Poor wretched one, poor wretch.
Ooze with the fresh showers into the rills of earth –
In vain you bathe your own face in your self,
It can be cleansed only in that of others.
Be the tiny blade upon the grass:
Greater than the spindle of the whole world's mass.
        O you machines, birds, tree-branches, constellations!
Our barren mother cries out for a child.
My friend, you dear, you most beloved friend,
Whether it comes in horror or in grandeur,
It is no shriek of mine, but the earth's thunder.

[early 1924]

With a Pure Heart

Fatherless and motherless,
godless in my statelessness,
neither crib nor shroud have I,
kiss nor lover's lullaby.

Three days, three, I've fasted three –
what is bread to such as me?
My twenty years shall prevail,
my twenty years are up for sale.

If nobody wants to buy,
devil take them then, say I.
With a pure heart I would steal,
if it needed, I could kill.

Catch me, hang me on a tree –
earth is blessed that covers me;
grave-grass on my heart yet grows,
heart as lovely as a rose.

[March 1925]

Because of this poem, József lost his good standing at Szeged University.
See Zsuzsanna Ozsváth's introduction, p.19.

Song of Young Women

We're the girlthings, chins of rounded
fuzzy mischief, shapely-headed, fleet-foot, whitely shoulder-bladed,
with our eyes and mouths complete.

While the dancing fire we're making, cooking, baking,
and our face with heat is aching, so the braided, shining-breaded
egg-loaf may refine its pleat.

Even the chaste wind is flirting, gets a feel of breastbuds slender,
        gently blowing
where our fragrance carries, lifting, fluttering our belled and glowing
        skirts about us.

We are busy cleaning, dusting, in a bun we tie our tresses,
stepping, stepping, topknot bounces, as a cock its comb it tosses.

And our fresh waists we are swinging, elbows', bottoms' rock and
        swaying,
as in dewy meadows dozens, scores of fat and happy babies,
naked, screaming, rolling over, over, in a heap were playing.

When our lords return at nightfall, we are waiting there with water,
        supper, kisses,
Tease him from his griefs with laughter, soothe his spirit worry-worn,
love him all the night, and after
watch our little bellies growing in the magic of the dawn.

[July–August 1925]

Sitting, Standing, Killing, Dying

Push the chair away uncaring,
squat before the train despairing,
scale a mountain tactically,
shake my bag into the valley,
feed a bee to my old spider,
stroke an old crone, sit beside her,
eat a bowl of good hot chowder,
tiptoe through the muddy weather,
lay my hat on railway metal,
skirt a lake, or sink and settle
clothed, to the bottom, far from troubles,
roasting in its tinkling bubbles –
bloom with every sunflower's petal,
or just sigh a thing of beauty,
or just drive off a bluebottle,
dust my books when they get dirty –
spit upon my mirror's middle,
sign my enemies' peace treaty,
kill them, knife them without pity,
analyse the blood's swift trickle,
watch a girl turn, sweet and fickle –
or just sit in silent numbers,
or burn Budapest to embers,
feed a bird with crumbs and butter,
hurl my stale bread to the gutter,
leave my loving sweetheart weeping,
grab her younger sister, groping,
and, if world is my accounting,
leave it, owing, unrelenting –

ah, you binding and dissolving,
you whose poem this is, evolving,
you, my laughing and my crying,
life, my choosing unto dying!

[Summer 1926]

Introduction

This is aunt Lidi's sister's son,
Budapest kin of Batu Khan,
who lived on bread since he was one,
had no blue-quilted eiderdown;
whose poems, with beans boiled in his cauldron,
death does not hesitate to buy;
hey, bourgeois, proletarian!
Attila József here stand I!

[May 1927]

This Is My Blessing, Sad and Merry

This is my blessing, sad and merry,
here is my heart's care, all I carry,
palms of beseeching guard your doings,
wheatlands and clouds your comings, goings.

The music at your footfalls crumbles,
my wall against you always tumbles,
rocked in its shadowy unwreathing,
I wrap myself within your breathing.

No matter if you love or leave me,
if heart shares heart, or you deceive me,
I still will see you, hear you, sing you,
as answer to God's questions, bring you.

At dawn the forest yawns and stretches,
and with its thousand arms it reaches
up to the sky to steal the lightness
and robe its loving heart with brightness.

[Christmas 1927]

70

Attila József

Merry and good, but obstinate
he was with doubters of his vision.
He loved to eat; his disposition
resembling God's in this and that;
from a Jewish doctor got
his coat; his relatives thereat
called him: Don't-Let-Me-See-Your-Face-Again.
In the Greek Orthodox religion
priests he found, but peace found not –
known through the country for destruction,

so there's no need to mourn a lot.

[early 1928]

Áron József Got Me

Áron József got me;
who beyond the Endless Sea,
soapmaker, forgot me;
now he mows the pungent hay.

Borcsa Pőcze bore me;
hellrot ate out her insides,
stomach, then her belly,
scrubbingbrush-legged centipedes.

Luce was my obsession;
but she didn't care for me.
All I own's illusion,
shadows all the friends I see.

No worse is there, never,
pain became my soul's address, –
I must live forever
idiotic, masterless.

[early 1928]

Luca Wallesz was one of József's early flames, a young woman who inspired many of his poems.

Rockabye

Still the gentle splashings,
rocking in the rushes,
halcyon unveilings,
blue lacustrine kisses.

Should her love awaken
with another, may it
rock her in her reedbed
as these ripples sway it.

[Spring 1928]

Lay Your Hand

Lay your hand
upon my brow
as if your hand
were my hand now.

Guard me as
my death would do,
guard me as if
my life were you.

Love me as if
it did you good
if my heart lay
where your heart stood.

[May–June 1928]

I Knew It

You were near, I knew it – by the way
every sunflower turned its stony head,
blowing where your coming footsteps led;
by our lettuce' ruffled disarray.

Mumbling: it's the windstorm of your dress!
it's a rill of bubbly poppycomb,
schools of golden fish the catspaws foam,
ryefields' rustle, smiling momentness.

Bath and ringing drink are you to me.
When upon my shoulder you will sigh,
then I know your arms' floodtide, and I
hear your breath break softly like the sea.

Rush between my teeth! In hot coals shiver!
Death is thirsty; I should drink you here:
summer is a great gold jug of beer,
chubby clouds the froths upon its river.

[June 1928]

Pearl

Pearl-star glimmers in its glow,
pearldrops scatter here below,
clustered grapes that break and roll,
water-globelets bright and cool.

I'm a burl of pallid soil,
brown, clodhopping, yet a pearl;
beaded on the furrowland,
flourish of the poor bare ground.

74

Starry hand to earthy head,
your frail star on my brow spread;
this my ham-hand on your heart,
turns to dust and falls apart.

Earth to earth I fall to dust,
frail star falls, as fall it must;
and the sky's a pearl again,
two hearts threaded on one skein.

[July 1928]

Beads

Beads around your neck aglow,
frogheads in the lake below.
Lambkin droppings,
lambkin droppings in the snow.

Rose within the moon's halo,
gold belt round your waist to go.
Hempen knottings
knotted round my neck just so.

Skirted legs so subtly swinging,
bell-tongue in its bell a-ringing,
river-mirror
with two swaying poplars' winging.

Skirted legs so subtly calling,
bell-tongue in its bell a-tolling,
river-mirror
with the dumb leaves falling, falling.

[Summer 1928]

Rime

My grapes, my purple clustering,
turn now to pea-pods festering.
Their tiny black eyes twirl and prickle,
mixed with my tears they fall and trickle.

Oh, pained and clumsy comings, goings,
my pale, windbroken, scrapings, bowings!
My scurrying, my knocking shoulder!
Scab of a maimed love left to moulder!

O bony chastity of heaven –
starved hoar-frost of a feast ungiven!
Unwinking, impeturbable!
Trusting that I'll do what is noble!

I live on diamond-chilly herring,
etheric furniture my dwelling,
my nails grow sharp and curve and harden,
their roses whiten in their garden.

[16 November 1928]

Medallions

1

I was an elephant, humble and meek,
I sucked the cool wise waters in my cheek,
I stood upon a hill midnight and noon
and fondled with my trunk the sun and moon –

then to their lips I offered up the tree,
the green horned beetle, snake, chalcedony, –
and now my soul: heaven's vanished with the years,
I fan myself with my enormous ears – –

2

On the frail drop of dew a dust-mote crawls,
I cover with my hands pants full of holes,
the little swineherd weeps and hugs alone
his pied piglet enchanted into stone –

the green-smoke sky slowly begins to flush,
clang, clang, the bell upon the lake's dull hush,
a milk-white flower is frozen in the ice,
on a parted leaf floats the universe – –

3

Toddle, toddle, little leech-fisherman,
gaze, gaze, poor skinny swineherd in the sun,
float, float, dark heron blue above the mere,
steam, steam, fresh cowpat fallen here –

up there, a fagged-out apple hangs on high,
into its heart a worm has chewed an eye,
thence it looks out, sees all things in their power,
a flower was this poem, an apple-flower – –

4

Perhaps you're foam on top of sugared milk,
perhaps, a night-sound's petrifying hulk,
perhaps, a knife in water, cold as lead,
perhaps a button torn off from its thread –

into the leaven falls the housemaid's tear,
no need to search for kisses, home is here,
you still can find it, lamplight shows the way,
kindling its smoky eyes, now don't delay – –

5

A god encarved of wood I sit upon,
a pig, whose knuckle is of jasper-stone,
hey, velvet grief-foam, on the milk be set!,
in death, my beard of hundredweights grows yet –

and if my skin still twitches, heavens above,
it's all that trickles through from spine to nave,
the little fatties in their glowing swarms,
the stars and galaxies, the small white worms – –

6

The greenish lizard seeks my fate, he gleams,
the knocking wheat ear casts its seed of dreams,
a stone falls in the lake, which looks at me,
and all the clouds the sighed-out mourners sigh,

the dawns commissioned in their sky-fought wars,
the leaping suns and finely-trembling stars,
around my quiet and sleepy head are hurled,
my temperature's the glowing of the world – –

7

Upon the step an iron-foamed pail is found,
wastewater spreading flatly on the ground, –
oh, love the barefoot girl who mops the stair,
the bubbled scum dried on her arms so bare –

I too am stamped into iron filigree,
but clattering through the horses of the sea
there's a free foaminess that rises, clangs
upon the stairwells' ranged and gleaming fangs – –

8

Attorney, frozen in an amber ball,
crouches in his frock coat, peers at it all,
transfixed he sees the care with which the light,
wind, fog, can cover, stroke, bless with delight.

run over by the rose, I moulder down,
but plucked by herons into eiderdown,
I am what warms the autumn night's first cold,
and keep the goosebumps from the frail and old – –

9

I have a friend who lives with me in bed,
no wilting lily under this bedspread,
I have no tommy-gun, no stone, no bow,
I'd like to kill though, as we all would so,

and while the haughty beans bubble and fry
with vegetable eyes you see how I
quiver and rock in fever my broad lips,
and swallows feed me still with gnats and thrips – –

10

Crackle, my beard, sizzle, come curling out,
a harrow for the crops, be dragged about –
skyover, cloudunder floats a caress,
a stroking, masterless, possessionless;

and this cool charm dragged gently to and fro
will one day rest upon my beard, and flow
and trickle down its red braid to my bunion,
a steamy tonic wine, a spiced communion – –

11

Twenty-three kings parade, so grand,
on their heads are jasper crowns,
eating cantaloupes of gold,
new moon bakes in their left hand.

Twenty-three kids wend by the land,
on their coxcombs hats of clowns,
supping melons what they hold,
new sun flames in their right hand – –

12

The black one, with the ever-trampled nose,
the yellow one, whose sky the bluer glows,
the redskin, laced with frozen blood so bright,
and, will-o'-the-skipping-wisp, the fog-born white –

– – – – – – – – – –
– – – – – – – – – –
– – – – – – – – – –
– – – – – – – – – –

[1927-28]

Tiszazug *(see poem on page 81)* is a village in the Hungarian lowlands where
a bizarre court case took place in 1929 that shocked the country to its core.
A large number of women were accused and found guilty of poisoning their
abusive husbands, fathers or sons with the help of a midwife. The killings
went on unnoticed for decades.

Tiszazug

Pine needles tack the sheepskin shade.
Upon the ice-crust rap the paws
of time's swift instant and glissade,
a Puli-dog with clicking claws.

The people mumble, dimly yearn;
the little houses brood, and watch:
over their windows, taciturn,
they pull their greasy caps of thatch.

The hen clucks sadly in its roost
under the gutter's sheltered lee,
as if she were the old hag's ghost
that haunts the place beseechingly.

Indoors more freckled livestock lurk,
bluish old loonies, addledly,
who grunt aloud at times, and jerk,
to stop the flow of reverie.

Because indeed there's much to brood
when there's no hoeing to be done.
The sweet soft gossip-pipes are chewed,
a thread in broken fingers spun.

For what's an old one worth? He drops
his spoon, he drools, is fed; so frail
that if he serves the piglets' slops
they knock him down and spill the pail.

And soft's the homestead, warm the pen.
The nightfall dangles from a star!
Hard is the firmament. A wren
limps peeping in a pine-bough's scar.

[Summer 1929]

Summer

Marigold horizons lie
over billowing meadow-leas,
silver in the floating sky
halcyon birch tree shakes the breeze.

Now the waspwaist wasp arrives,
sniffs and grunts, squats on a rose.
Cumbered, the angry crimson writhes –
on, yet, the slim young summer goes.

Still more, still yet, the welling grows.
Strawberries blood-rich on the loam
drowse in the warm, the eared wheat blows.
Crouched in the boughs, a thunderstorm.

So swift my summer is fulfilled!
On flying witch-balls rides the gale –
sky claps and flashes, sudden, chilled,
with fairy light from winter's pale.

[Summer 1929/1934]

The Woodcutter

I split a cord of chilly timber,
knots gleam and shriek in brightening timbre,
frost wings my hair with hoary feather,
tickles my neck in the cold weather –
     on velvet now my minutes run.

High up, frost's glittering axe-head flashes,
all sparkles, earth, sky, eyes, brow, lashes,
dawn whoops, light flicks away in splinters –
the woodman grunts and chops; these winters
     I cut the branch but not the trunk.

– Ay, break the stock without misgiving,
nor fret for every chip and shaving,
if you strike out at fate, then surely
the lordly owned land screams with fury –
     the broad bright axe-blade strokes and smiles.

[November 1929; February 1931]

The Kings of Bethlehem

Gentle Jesus, gloria, gloria!
We three kings of orient are,
    star above us blazing, blazing,
    hurried here to join the praising,
    for a tiny sheep, to please us,
    told us, here must live our Jesus.
        I am Melchior the king,
        Save me, dearest heavenling!

In excelsis, Lord of Hosts, Lord of Hosts!
We are not some dry old priests.
    What we heard was at your borning,
    kingdom of the poor was dawning.
    We looked in for just a glimmer,
    heavenly king and our redeemer!
        Caspar's what my name would be,
        sort of earthly king, you see.

Deo gratia, Son of Man, Son of Man!
We are from the sunny land,
    all our sausages long eaten,
    twinkly boots collapsed and beaten,
    bring six handfuls' gold from Asia,
    incense in an iron brazier.
        I am the one named Balthazar,
        of Saracens the emperor.

Flushing-blushing Mary-girl, Mary-girl!
Blessèd mother, flower and pearl,
    through her tears in showers falling,
    scarcely sees her Jesus-darling;
    hears the shepherds' drum and piper,
    but the baby needs his supper.
        Dearest kings so fine and bright,
        now I wish you all good night!

[December 1929]

In Memory of Ady

– He died? Then why do they still kill him daily
with words, with actions, even with a hush?
Why do the smooth ones cleverly and slyly
reduce his wrath to a girl's pouting blush?
Magyar on Magyar soil, poet within it,
he grasps in angry fists two clods of earth,
above his breast the cloud rears infinite:
but still his revolutions come to birth.

He works on, unforgetting, unassuaging,
there in the strange dark dwellings of the ground,
a thousand acres thunder with his raging,
he hunts the steppes, drives the winds round and round –
those cruel winds which at their lordly pleasure
scatter the little scratched-up ricks of hay,
and with their blast rip snow and thatch together
from Dózsa's folk in sunken hamlets grey.

His body is the soil's. His soul the digger's,
whose hoe beats sometimes with a deep refrain.
His grave's the freehold of three million beggars,
where they may build, and plant, and reap the grain.
His verse is law; and to the drum of Ady
the hurled stones strike, the castle windows rend, –
the plough cuts one more furrow in his body
whose life will flower forever without end.

[23 March 1930]

Endre Ady (1877-1918) was one of Hungary's greatest poets.
György Dozsa (1470-1514), the leader of a failed peasant revolt, was executed
by the aristocracy.

On a Poet

Yapping jackal, croaking raven,
shamed, the prince of sneers
blurts his song, the filthy craven,
master but of years.
    Less than a leech, he mocks his psalms
    who dreams not of his hothouse palms.

May then his palms by curs be watered,
and may the gardener too.
As autumn's ripe manure is scattered,
be mulched with doggy-doo.
    And as he excavates his nose,
    imagine that he feels his muse.

Why, letching after rings of vapour,
with his winged ass amain,
fights he not as man and shaper
with the people's pain?
    – beats his fogs to mouldy creamings,
    cannot stir the stormcloud's dreamings?

What's to him the wound and grieving
of our folk so dear,
tattered like a cloud unweaving
in the winds of fear.
    We like threadworms drift thereunder,
    torn by lordly strokes of thunder...

His soul's a husk of empty hustle
gemmed with a little frog.
Croaking while the profits rustle,
toadying in the bog.
    An emerald at any distance,
    better not touch his slime-existence.

...Sold cheap, that soul, as ailments are,
with well-earned modesty.
Let us bestow upon our star
this od'rous rose, perdy.
    O what a thunder maketh he:
    his little tummy's colicky.

[April 1930]

With this poem, József launched an unfortunate attack against **Mihály Babits**
(1883-1941), a major figure in Hungarian poetry. See details in Zsuzsanna
Ozsváth's introduction, pp.23-26.

Chant

Once I milked a soot-nosed bull,
    foxtale, hide and seek,
in bull's milk my fate to tell,
    foxtale, hide and seek.
In my seven pails' good steel,
    foxtale, hide and seek,
milkfoam gan to flame and flail,
    foxtale, hide and seek.
So to hide my flaming pail,
    foxtale, hide and seek,
plucked I roses pink and pale,
    foxtale, hide and seek.
People's rye rocks in the rose,
    foxtale, hide and fell,
bailiff's heart in cabbage-rows,
    foxtale, hide and fell.
Bailiff strokes his lord with oils,
    foxtale, hide and fell,
pays the folk with posts and rails,
    foxtale, hide and fell.
May his hay turn into straw,
    foxtale, hide and fell,
leeches for his noodle-slaw,
    foxtale, hide and fell.

Let their goatshorns turn to fire,
      foxtale, hide and fell,
pierce the quilt and burn the mire,
      foxtale, hide and fell.

[April 1930]

Grief

Like unto a stag I fled,
soft grief made my eyes to smart.
Forest-gnawing wolves unfed
hunt each other in my heart.

Antler broken yesteryear,
lost, swings idle on the bough.
I that whilom was a deer
to my grief a wolf am now.

I a bonny wolf became.
Spellstruck, though, I halt stockstill,
wolf-companions froth and foam;
painfully I try to smile,

listen to the sweet-voiced doe,
for a dream I close my eye:
mulberry-leaves fall dark and slow
on my shoulder, where they lie.

[June 1930]

What Will Become of Him...

What will become of him, whoever
has got no handle to his hoe,
upon whose whiskers crumbs don't quiver,
who dawdles, gloomy, thrawn, and slow;
who would from half a furlong's hoeing
keeps one potato out of three,
whose hair falls out in patches, growing
bald unnoticed – who'd care to see?

What will become of him, whoever
has but five acres under crops,
whose draggled hen clucks at the stover,
whose thoughts nest in a mudhole's slops;
when no yoke clinks, no oxen bellow;
when mother serves the family soup
and steam from liquid weak and yellow
drifts in the bottom of the scoop?

What will become of him, whoever
must live alone and work alone;
whose stew has neither salt nor savour,
the grocer gives no tick nor loan;
who has one broken chair for kindling,
cat sitting on the cracked stove's shelf;
who sets his key-chain swinging, jingling,
who stares, stares; lies down by himself?

What will become of him, whoever
works to support his family;
the cabbage-heart they quarrel over,
the film the big girl gets to see;
always the laundry – dirt's slow strangling –
the wife's mouth tastes of vegetables,
and when the light's off, silent wrangling,
gropings, eavesdroppings, darkness, rules?

What will become of him, whoever
idles outside the factory,
a woman meanwhile hauls the lever,
a pale-skulled child sets the fusee;
when through the gates he gazes vainly,
vainly humps bags and market-creels –
he dozes, they rouse him inhumanely,
and always catch him when he steals?

What will become of him, whoever
weighs out potatoes, salt, and bread,
wraps them in newsprint's inky flavour,
and doesn't brush the scales he's read;
and in the gloom he dusts, complaining,
the rent is high, the tax is keen,
the price – but what's the use explaining
the extra charge for kerosene?

And what will come of him, whoever
knows he's a poet, sings his fears,
whose wife mops up the floor forever,
who chases copy-work for years;
whose name's a brand-name, if he has one,
just like a soap or cooking fat,
whose life is given, if he has one,
all to the proletariat?

[January 1932]

90

Night in the Outskirts

From loading-yards like deep sea caves
the light now lifts its sagging net,
our kitchen's drowned beneath the waves,
sunk in a dusk still darker yet.

Silence, – a scrub-brush almost goes
languidly to its feet, to crawl;
a bit of brick wall dimly knows
that it must either stand or fall.

Tattered, oil-soaked, now the evening
sighs in the sky and quits,
at the town's edge exhausted sits;
across the square it staggers, yawning,
then lights a bit of moon for burning.

Like ruins of the dusk they rise,
factories,
but still,
of deeper darkness yet they are the mill,
foundations of silence.

And through their windows flies in sheaves
the moonlight's frieze,
its mysteries:
out of whose woof each ribbed loom weaves
till dawn, when workaday resumes,
sombrely out of gloom and gleams
the sleeping mill-girls' tumbled dreams.

A vaulted graveyard looms beyond:
lime-kiln, iron-mill, screw-mill, silent.
Family crypts whose echoes' fiction
guards a secret resurrection:
closely whispered mysteries.
A cat investigates the fence,
a watchman, superstitious, sees
a sudden flash, will-o'-the-wisp

that glows and blinks and vanishes, –
the beetle-bodied dynamos
shine cool, obscure, immense.

Train whistle.

Dew infiltrates the dusk, and sleeves
a fallen linden's greying leaves:
dust in the roadway
clogs as it cleaves.

A muttering worker, cop upon his beat.
Comrade, with leaflets, cuts across the street.
Just as a dog
sniffs and follows what's before him,
as a cat turns back and hearkens,
circling streetlights, where it darkens.

The inn's mouth spews out light that's rotten,
its windows vomit pools of ache;
inside, the choked lamp swings forgotten,
a labourer keeps a lonely wake.
The barman wheezes in his doze;
the drunk grins at the wall's illusion,
reels on the lewd stairs, overflows,
weeps. And cheers the revolution.

The clapping water sets and chills
like smeltings in the mills.
The wind moves like a dog astray,
its great tongue touches, loose and splay,
the waters; drinks and swills.

Hay-mattresses like rafts swim mute
upon the serried waves of dark –

The warehouse is a shipwrecked bark,
the foundry's an iron barge: behold
the foundryman dreams through the mould
a scarlet babe of molten gold.

All's thick with dew, all's heaviness.
The mildew traces out the maps
of all the lands of wretchedness.
The barren fields of tattered grass
yield only rags and paper scraps.
They'd crawl if but they could. They stir,
too feeble to do more.

In whose image the soiled laundry flaps,
blown by your moist and clinging air,
O Night!
as ragged sheets hung out to dry
on life's worn clothesline of the sky,
O Grief, O Night!
Night of the poor! become my coal,
smoke hotly here upon my soul,
melt from my heart its steel, make it
the standing anvil that won't split,
the hammer's twang and glit colliding, –
in victory the forged blade gliding,
O Night!

I sleep, brothers, that I might be fresh.
The night is heavy, somber, whole.
Let not the worm devour our flesh.
Let not affliction crush our soul.

[1932]

The Last of Seven

Mortal dweller, may your mother
bear you seven times together!
Once within a house that's burning,
once in floods, the icefloes churning,
once in bedlam, yelling, yearning,
once in a wheatfield's soft turning,
once in cloisters bell-intoning,
once stied with pigs in grunts and groaning.
What though these six cry out to heaven?
You shall be the last of seven!

If your enemy come to hurt you,
seven there be who won't desert you:
one who starts his day off ready,
one who's on his tour of duty,
one who takes no pay for teaching,
one cast onto the waves, beseeching,
one, a seed of forests splendid,
one, bellowing ancestors defended
when all his tricks could not get even –
you shall be the last of seven!

If you're seeking for a woman,
seven seek her love in common.
One who spends his heart upon her,
one who pays his debts of honour,
one who plays the musing dreamer,
one who gropes her skirt, the schemer,
one knows where the hook is hidden,
one treads her kerchief, that's forbidden, –
as flies buzz meat, their goal and heaven!
You shall be the last of seven!

94

If you'd make a poet's living,
seven will work the poem-giving.
One build towns of marble vision,
one born sleeping, a magician,
one who measures heaven's gutters,
one whose name the logos utters,
one who carves his soul a tiller,
one vivisector and rat-killer.
Four scientists, two heroes even –
you shall be the last of seven!

And if it falls as it is written,
seven to the grave are smitten:
one dandled at a milk-filled bosom,
one grasping at a stony bosom,
one who scorns the empty platters,
one ally of the poor, in tatters,
one worn to shreds by work and action,
one gazer at the moon's perfection:
may you share the tomb of heaven!
You shall be the last of seven!

[1932]

Winter Night

Discipline, discipline!

Summer's pyre
has lost its fire.
Above the cinders of its origin
trembles the slight ash of what has been.
A quiet place.
The air's
lens, its flawless glass
is scratched where two sharp hawthorn branches cross.
Beautiful inhumanity. A trace
of slender silver – tattered ribbon – dangles
stiffened against the briar's cruel tangles,
caught, with so many a smile and a caress
on the world's branchiness.

The gnarled old mountains bordering these lands
hold within exhausted hands
trembling with age and heaviness,
the hearth, the evening fire,
the steaming homestead pale,
the breathing moss, the round quiet of the vale.

Heavy now, the labourer's homeward bound,
his members all stare at the ground.
Upon his shoulder plods the broken hoe,
its handle bleeds, its iron bleeds as they go.
As if from his existence he trudged home,
limbs getting heavier with the climb,
tools getting heavier all the time.

And now the sky ascends, like smoke from stacks,
its glittering stars in shoals and packs.

The blue iron night comes rolling through the sky's still shell,
tolled by the sombre-gonging bell.
As if the heart would sempiternally be still,
and something else, not transience, nor
our mortality, should pulse the landscape with its spell.

As if the winter night, the winter sky, the winter ore
had been the bell,
and its tongue the earth reforged, its heavy swing its choice.
And heart the voice.

Memory hears the floating clang. Mind hears it too.
The winter's forged an anvil, there to shoe
the iron-braced barrel-vault, its hanging door,
where fruit, wheat, light, straw all summer long pour through,
and there is always more.

As fairy-glittering as thought, as bright,
twinkles the winter night.

Darkness' silver silence locks
the moon onto the Earth's still parallax.

A black crow flies across the frostcold sky;
silence cools in my mouth. Bone, do you hear it?
Molecules tinkle, crystals ramify.

In what glass case or cabinet
glitter such winter nights?
against the frost the branch's dagger's set,
and in regret
the plainlands heave a shuddering sigh – –
through the low fog hosts of crows fleet by.

Winter night. Across the plain,
like its own small winter night,
a freight train sets its plume of smoke alight.,
chora to contain
in a cord's bourne, infinite,
the turning, burning, dying stars' domain.

Along the freight cars' roofs of hoary white
scurries a little mouse of winter light,
the dark light of the night's terrain.

Above the cities' dreams
the winter steams and steams.

But on the blue frost of the rails
night's yellow gleaming flits and trails
into the city's glow again.

That rigid, stultifying light of night
has pitched its workshop in the city's spite
to manufacture blades of pain.

Out in the city's pales
like wet straw falls the lamplight, and impales
a rattling coat
hunched at a corner, lonely and remote,
a man, whose body quails,
huddles like the Earth into a ball, in vain,
for winter's stepped upon his feet...

Where a tree with rusty leaves leans in,
down from the encircling gloom,
I measure this, the winter night.
An owner might
thus measure his domain.

[December 1932]

Beyond Hope

Slowly, musingly

I am as one who comes to rest
by that sad, sandy, sodden shore
and looks around, and undistressed
nods his wise head, and hopes no more.

Just so I try to turn my gaze
with no deceptions, carelessly.
A silver axe-swish lightly plays
on the white leaf of the poplar tree.

Upon a branch of nothingness
my heart sits trembling voicelessly,
and watching, watching, numberless,
the mild stars gather round to see.

In heaven's iron-blue vault...

In heaven's iron-blue vault revolves
a cool and lacquered dynamo.
The word sparks in my teeth, resolves
– oh, noiseless constellations! – so –

In me the past falls like a stone
through space as voiceless as the air.
Time, silent, blue, drifts off alone.
The sword-blade glitters; and my hair –

My moustache, a fat chrysalis,
tastes on my mouth of transience.
My heart aches, words cool out to this.
To whom, though, might their sound make sense?

[March 1933]

On the Edge of the City

Where I live, on the edge of the city,
behold as dusk caves in
like bats on insubstantial membranes
the soft soot glide and spin
and settle, as the layers of guano do
in a thick, horny skin.

So sits this age upon the spirit.
And as the heavy rain
in tatters goes on washing, washing
the chipped tin roof and drain,
so grief wipes at the heart's sclerosis
over and over again.

Blood could get it clean – that's how we are.
New folk, another breed.
Our accent's strange, our hair clings strangely
to a different head.
Not God, nor even thoughts, but coal
and oil and iron instead,

the real material, created us
and poured us, fiery-found,
into the iron moulds of society,
the ghoul that holds us bound,
that we might be the conscience of the human
on the eternal ground.

After the priests, the warriors, and the burghers,
thus we became the true,
the ultimate, observer of the laws;
all man makes that is new,
creation's essence, therefore thrums in us,
as deep violas do.

Never so many, though the past lies deep
since sun and planets formed,
have wrecked and wasted the imperishable:
famine and war have stormed

our dwellings, blind beliefs and cholera
have gathered, grown, and swarmed.

Under the stars the designated one,
he who shall inherit,
was never yet so shamed and cast so low
as you who now bear it:
our eyes are thrown down to the ground. The earth
opens, reveals its secret.

Just look at it, the pretty, precious pet,
the machine run amok!
The fragile villages, like weak ice, bend
cracking under the shock,
the cities' plaster slides as the sky leaps
with thunder's shattering knock.

And who – the squire, perhaps? – will dare scold down
the shepherd's savage hound?
Its childhood was our childhood. To our flesh
was the machine bred and bound.
It eats out of our hand. Go ahead, scold!
We know its name and ground.

And now we see already how you stumble
and fall upon your knees
and pray to what you barely can possess
but never shall appease.
But it obeys but him who fed it, will
no other master please...

Behold us then, here suspect and together,
matter's first offspring.
Lift up our heart! For it belongs to him
who raises it to sing.
He only can be strong who has been filled
with our inspiriting.

Lift up our heart, above the factories!
great sooty heart, as vast
as only he can know who's seen the sun
choke in its overcast,

who's heard the the throbbing in the earth's deep shafts,
its echoing exhaust!

Up, up! ... around this chartered and divided land
the picket fence complains,
staggers, is dizzy with the violence of our breathing,
like stormwinds on the plains.
Let's blow it all away! Lift up your heart,
set fire to heaven's domains!

Till it lights up our lovely sense of order,
that urge to shapeliness
by which the brain knows and acknowledges
finite unboundedness:
the outward forces of production and the inward
instinctive drive to bliss...

The city's edge sirens this wordless song.
The poet, worker's kin,
watches, can only watch, the fall, the fall,
the fat soot glide and spin,
that settles, as the layers of guano do,
in a hard, horny skin.

The poet – the word may rattle on his lips,
but he (the engineer
who serves the magic of the given world),
seeing the future clear,
as you without, so he within – constructs
a new harmonic sphere.

[Spring 1933]

102

Elegy

As smoke pack thickly drifts under a leaden sky
across the face of this sad region,
so floats my mind's eye,
sinking, sliding.
But not gliding.

Hard soul and soft imagination!
Retracing thus the harsh tracks of reality
to your self self, to your nativity,
come down and see!
Here beneath a once swift-flowing sky
a sullen poverty
trapped amid these sheetwalls' haggard loneliness,
by mute threats and pleading silences
dissolves the thickened pain
in the sensitive man's heart and brain
and mingles it
with that of millions.

An entire human world
is here preparing. All's but ruins yet. A hard-
head dandelion pops its umbrella
in the empty factory yard.
By faded stairs of small cracked window-panes
the daylight sinks toward the drains
into the darkening below.
Answer:
Are you from here?
Never able to get clear
of sombre yearning to possess
what all the wretched of the earth must bear,
in whom an age of greatness they can't know
is pent, their faces warped to ugliness?

You rest here in the empty yards
where this crippled paling guards
with screech and scream
the pigs' régime.

Recognise yourself? These souls await
some better-founded future, workmanly
and beautiful; they wait as empty as the state
of vacant lots around them, in their dreaming
– sombre and musing as they well may be –
of mansions tall with their rooms a-spin and teeming.
With fixed eyes lustreless the shards of glass
stuck in the dried mud stare and see
the aching hedges that still fence them in.
The sandpiles sometimes spill a thimbleful
of sand... and one by one, zigzagging, plausible,
the buzzing flies arrive, green, black, and blue,
drawn here by the human residue
and tatters,
from richer climes and riper matters.
Here too in its own ways the table's set
by usury-tormented,
blessed mother earth.
Yellow grass blooms yet in an iron pot.

Do you know
what barren mental joy you undergo
that pulls you so, that you can not get free,
what rich and subtle agony
attracts you so?
To his mother thus returns the child
by strangers shoved and beaten and reviled.
Truthfully
here only may you smile and may you cry.
Here you've yourself for company.
O soul! This is your country.

[Spring 1933]

Ode

1

I am alone on these glittering crags.
A sinuous breeze
floats delicious, the infant summer's
suppertime simmer and ease.
I school my heart into this silence.
Not so arduous –
All that is vanished is aswarm in me,
my head is bowed, and my hand is
vacuous.

I see the mane of the mountain –
each little leafvein
leaps with the light of your brow.
The path is quite deserted,
I see how your skirt is floated
in the wind's sough.
Under the tender, the tenuous bough
I see you shake out your hair, how it clings,
your soft, trembling breasts; behold
– just as the Szinva-stream glides beneath –
the round white pebbles of your teeth,
and how the welling laughter springs
tumbling over them like fairy gold.

2

Oh how much I love you, who've given
speech to both the universes:
the heart's caves, its trickweaving deepenings,
sly involute lonelinesses –
and starry heaven.
As water glides from its own thunderous fall
you fly from me and we are cleft and parted,
whilst I, among the mountains of my life, still call,
still kneel, and sing, and raise the echo with my cry,
slamming against the earth and sky,
that I love you, step-nurse, mother-hearted!

3

I love you as a child his mother's breast,
as the dumb caves their own bottomlessness,
as halls the light that shows them best,
as the soul loves flame, as the body rest!
I love you as we who marked for death
love the moments of their living breath.

Every smile, every word, every move you make,
as falling bodies to my earth, I press;
as into metal acids eat and ache,
I etch you in my brains with instinct's stress,
beautiful shapeliness,
your substance fills the essence they partake.

The moments march by, clattering and relentless,
but in my ears your silence lies.
Even the stars blaze up, fall, evanesce,
but you're a stillness in my eyes.
The taste of you, hushed like a cavern-pool,
floats in my mouth, as cool;
your hand, upon a water-glass,
veined with its glowing lace,
dawns beautiful.

4

Ah, what strange stuff is this of which I'm made,
that but your glance can sculpt me into shape? –
what kind of soul, what kind of light or shade,
what prodigy that I, who have long strayed
in my dim fog of nothingness unmade,
explore your fertile body's curving scape?

– And as the logos flowers in my brain,
immerse myself in its occult terrain!...

Your capillaries, like a blood-red rose,
ceaselessly stir and dance.
There that eternal current seethes and flows
and flowers as love upon your countenance,
to bless with fruit your womb's dark excellence.

106

A myriad rootlets broider round
and round your stomach's tender ground,
whose subtle threadings, woven and unwound,
unknit the very knot whereby they're bound,
that thus thy lymphy cellbrood might abound,
and the great, leaved boughs of thy lungs resound
their whispered glory round!

The *eterna materia* goes marching on
happily through your gut's dark cavern-cells,
and to the dead waste rich life is given
within the ardent kidneys' boiling wells!

Billowing, your hills arise, arise,
constellations tremble in your skies,
lakes, factories work on by day and night,
a million creatures bustle with delight,
millipede,
seaweed,
a heartless mercy, gentle cruelty,
your hot sun shines, your darkling north light broods,
in you there stir the unscanned moods
of a blind incalculable eternity.

5

So falls in clotted spatters
at your feet this blood,
this parched utterance.
Being stutters;
law is the only spotless eloquence.
My toiling organs, wherein I am renewed
over and over daily, are subdued
to their final silence.

But yet each part cries out –
O you who from the billioned multitude,
O you unique, you chosen, wooed
and singled out, you cradle, bed,
and grave, soft quickener of the dead,
receive me into you!...

(How high is this dawn-shadowy sky!
Armies are glittering in its ore.
Radiance anguishing to the eye.
Now I am lost, I can no more.
Up in the world I hear it batter,
my heart's old roar.)

6 (ENVOI)

(Now the train's going down the track,
maybe today it'll carry me back,
maybe my hot face will cool down today,
maybe you'll talk to me, maybe you'll say:

Warm water's running, there's a bath by and by!
Here is a towel, now get yourself dry!
The meat's on the oven, and you will be fed!
There where I lie, there is your bed.)

[June 1933]

Szinva is the name of a brook in the Bükk Mountains.

(Self-devouring, haggard Virtue!...)

Self-devouring, haggard Virtue!
I have hurt you.

You carved a stick with runes, your craft
taught language to its haft,
then, bored, you let it drop. Was it not so?
Just so the firmament will throw
a worn-out star down through the darks of space.
I picked it up and hit you in the face.

Was it not so?
The pity of it, and the woe.

The birdsong of your new-dreamed dream, it was
as if, in my own world, I heard it but through glass,
recognised only such dull strains
as can seep through the heavy panes
of loneliness.
And in that song I heard confess
a voice that spoke of gods who now refuse
to bow down to your muse;
but You
had already left their retinue.

At last I understand.
Those who contend
stand face to face as we did, but you too
upon another case, another ground,
bore witness, as I did, to what's true.

And so I understand. What's that to you?
The past's parade has been and gone,
the leaves fall down,
and pain's stark branches turn to stone,
just as in all of us, the falling years,
the seasons and decades in sheets and layers,
congeal to strata, strewn bones turned to lime
beneath the enormous weight of time.

See the discussion of the relationship between József and Babits in Zsuzsanna
Ozsváth's introduction, pp.23-26.

Just like split firewood stacked together,
the universe embraces all,
so that each object holds the other
confined by pressures mutual,
all things ordained, reciprocal.
Just so the rich, the poor, exist and die,
just so we suffer, you and I;
perhaps it's best if anger maul
not one's own, but the other's soul,
artist against artist,
piper against flautist,
I against you, you against me,
for how then would it be, how could it be,
if always at oneself would gnaw
intelligence's frightful claw?

And since I speak of it, I'll tell, –
how in a tram
on Szena Square one night it fell
that we once met. I raised my hat,
swallowed, perhaps, at that,
greeted you, saw how you turned your eyes,
noted me with surprise.

And there, confused,
for a time I idly mused –
how after all we might
have been good friends, how on this night
we could be bound for some café,
what I would say, what you would say,
how, stirring tea, we might pursue
the good, the beautiful, the true,
and talk of literary trends
and such important human odds and ends;
how I would mark the pregnant words you'd say,
which you judiciously would weigh,
alluding to your long experience;
how I'd be carried off with passion,
how you – while adding: 'please don't take offence' –
would raise your older hand in admonition,
as fathers do,
and I'd be vexed, but would not tell you so.

[June 1933]

110

Consciousness

1

The dawn dissevers earth and skies
and at its pure and lovely bidding
the children and the dragonflies
twirl out into the sunworld's budding;
no vapour dims the air's receding,
a twinkling lightness buoys the eyes!
Last night into their trees were gliding
the leaves, like tiny butterflies.

2

Blue, yellow, red, they flocked my dream,
smudged images the mind had taken,
I felt the cosmic order gleam –
and not a speck of dust was shaken.
My dream's a floating shade; I waken;
order is but an iron regime.
By day, the moon's my body's beacon,
by night, an inner sun will burn.

3

I'm gaunt, sometimes bread's all I touch,
I seek amid this trivial chatter
unrecompensed, and yearn to clutch,
what has more truth than dice, more matter.
No roast rib warms my mouth and platter,
no child my heart, foregoing such –
the cat can't both, how deft a ratter,
inside and outside make her catch.

4

Just like split firewood stacked together,
the universe embraces all,
so that each object holds the other
confined by pressures mutual,
all things ordained, reciprocal.
Only unbeing can branch and feather,
only becoming blooms at all;
what is must break, or fade, or wither.

5

Down by the branched marshalling-yard
I lurked behind a root, fear-stricken,
of silence was the living shard,
I tasted grey and weird-sweet lichen.
I saw a shadow leap and thicken:
it was the shadow of the guard –
did he suspect? – watched his shade quicken
upon the heaped coal dew-bestarred.

6

Inside there is a world of pain,
outside is only explanation.
the world's your scab, the outer stain,
your soul's the fever-inflammation.
Jailed by your heart's own insurrection,
you're only free when you refrain,
nor build so fine a habitation,
the landlord takes it back again.

7

I stared from underneath the evening
into the cogwheel of the sky –
the loom of all the past was weaving
law from those glimmery threads, and I
looked up again into the sky
from underneath the steams of dreaming
and saw that always, by and by,
the weft of law is torn, unseaming.

8

Silence gave ear: the clock struck one.
Maybe you could go back to boydom;
walled in with concrete dank and wan,
maybe imagine hints of freedom.
And now I stand, and through the sky-dome
the stars, the Dippers, shine and burn
like bars, the sign of jail and thraldom,
above a silent cell of stone.

9

I've heard the crying of the steel,
I've heard the laugh of rain, its pattern;
I've seen the past burst through its seal:
only illusions are forgotten,
for naught but love was I begotten,
bent, though, beneath my burdens' wheel –
why must we forge such weapons, flatten
the gold awareness of the real?

10

He only is a man, who knows
there is no mother and no father,
that death is only what he owes
and life's a bonus altogether,
returns his find to its bequeather,
holding it only till he goes;
nor to himself, nor to another,
takes on a god's or pastor's pose.

11

I've seen what they call happiness:
soft, blonde, it weighed two hundred kilos;
it waddled smiling on the grass,
its tail a curl between two pillows.
Its lukewarm puddle glowed with yellows,
it blinked and grunted at me – yes,
I still remember where it wallows,
touched by the dawns of blissfulness.

12

I live beside the tracks, where I
can see the trains pass through the station.
I see the brilliant windows fly
in floating dark and dim privation.
Through the eternal night's negation
just so the lit-up days rush by;
in all the cars' illumination,
silent, resting my elbow, I.

[January–June 1934]

Mother

The autumn drizzle's greyish bun,
hangs gasping in my face, undone.
She's wept three days, and still she'll sing,
like a mad mother muttering
– for I am yearning for the teat –
eyes fixed on me, I've found my sweet,
my child, my darling, hushabye,
sleep little sweetheart, hushabye...

[early September 1934]

Mama

I've thought one week of Mama only.
Upon her hips she bore, ungainly,
a clothes-basket; she'd climb the stairway
up to the drying-attic's airway.

Then, for I was an honest fellow,
how I would shriek and stamp and bellow!
That swollen laundry needs no mother.
Take me, and leave it to another.

But still she drudged so quietly,
nor scolded me nor looked upon me,
and the hung clothes would glow and billow
high up above, with swoop and wallow.

It's too late now to still my bother;
what a giant was my mother –
over the sky her grey hair flutters,
her bluing tints the heaven's waters.

[October 1934]

114

Dread

Eternal twilight shrouds the kitchen,
behind an alcove there's a cough:
lips pursed, in rags, uneasy, twitching,
a tiny infant dozes off.

A puddle on the frigid flagging
quivers as in an autumn wind.
A little girl sits twisted, sagging,
prying the corners of her mind.

alone these two must live forsaken,
by hatred and desire they're fed,
with Shag the dog, a faded icon
of Rákóczy above the bed.

The girl is seven. She'd flee, maybe:
here you can't even jump about.
But mother left her with this baby,
This dead brute with its filthy snout.

She would escape!..., instead she muses
almost to swooning in her chair.
The rage pent up in her amazes:
she could crush cities then and there.

...But there, his swollen eyes pop open,
the tiny boy-child starts to squall.
Her own eyes measure him, and deepen;
she warms his milk up, stoical.

Silently, rigidly, she watches
his face turned blue with want of air.
Its wing awry, a ribbon perches,
a dead moth in her livid hair.

Then shoves into the screamer's gullet
the bottle's teat, heavy and thick.
He coughs and chokes upon this bullet,
creaks tautly like a breaking stick.

His small frame ripples like an ocean;
the nipple drips, a leaking tap;
she plucks it out, a sudden motion;
he swallows, howls, and tries to grab.

And now, he'll gape and tense and struggle;
So once again she'll thrust it in,
But by the time he'll suck and nuzzle,
She'll pull it from his lips again.

The child can't know: should he go crazy
or cry forever with the pain?
His anger shakes him. Milk comes cheesy
up from his tummy, cakes his chin.

He's crimson as a newborn; writhing,
the veins like maggots crawl his head;
his leg goes out, helplessly striving,
his big toe stiffens in his bed.

He screams, would nurse, but gags with terror;
he gums the darkling air unfed;
not since the gods were born, such horror,
never to parents came such dread.

The child is clammy with the terror, –
if she would give, why take it back?
She's colder than a murderer.
Blind man sings in the cul-de-sac.

She plays thus, half an hour together,
silently, without a smile.
The woman from next door comes over;
the startled girl replies with guile:

'Maybe the poor wee thing is teething!'
called softly through the open crack;
Then sits down in the alcove, weaving
ten slender fingers round and back.

At night the mother – for weeks already
it's been this way – takes up her son;
he grasps at her, distracted, greedy,
but the sweet milk he will have none.

He cries when he perceives the bottle,
craves but her lap, so warm and dear;
shakes like an old and worn-out cripple,
closes his eyes against the fear.

The mother doesn't know what's happened
(she is still taking off her shawl).
The girl is plausible and glib-tongued:
'I fed him when I heard him call.

'Mummy, let me cook the supper!',
and gives a gay mock-sprightly wail.
Mummy collapses in a stupor,
weary for sleep, exhausted, frail.

At night the stars no longer sparkle,
tears fill the seasons and the sky.
Dreaming, she weeps; wakes with a startle,
thinks she has heard the baby cry.

His face congeals a silent whimper .
She gets up, sees his grin of pain –
a rictus stiffened to a simper,
and calmed, she falls asleep again...

At dawn she puts a snack together
then hurries off to work somehow.
The girl arises, sees her brother,
gets dressed and makes a solemn vow.

But left inside, no disobeying,
Loneliness, pain, call out for more;
The baby cries, she should be playing –
and all is as it was before.

[November 1934]

Ferenc Rákóczy II (1676-1735) was Prince of Transylvania and leader
of the War of Independence. He died in exile.

Lullaby

The sky's blue eyes are falling shut,
shut, too, the house's many eyes;
fields sleep beneath their coverlet –
so go to sleep now, little Blaise.

Ants rest their heads upon their knees,
the drowsy wasps are in a daze,
their business and buzzing cease –
so go to sleep now, little Blaise.

The streetcar snores, its rumbling
dozes, forgetful of the days,
but rings its dream-bell, ding-a-ling –
so go to sleep now, little Blaise.

Asleep the jacket on the chair,
its torn sleeve dozes where it lies,
this day no further will it tear –
so go to sleep now, little Blaise.

The whistle snoozes, and the ball,
the woods and picnic holidays,
the favourite choccie-bar, and all –
so go to sleep now, little Blaise.

Distance, glass marble of the skies,
you will achieve in all your ways,
you'll be a giant; close your eyes –
and go to sleep now, little Blaise.

A soldier, fireman, you will be!
shepherd, you'll lead wild game to graze!
Mummy herself drifts off, just see –
so go to sleep now, little Blaise.

[2 February 1935]

I Did Not Know

Sin always seemed to me a fairytale.
Such stupid words they taught, such foolish labels.
I laughed at them – they were so old and stale!
He prates of sin whom cowardice disables!

I did not know what monsters made their cave
within my heart. A child, in my illusions,
so rocked within its mother's arms and gave
back, pulsing in response, its dreams and visions.

But now I know. This quivering truth discloses
with its great light the primal crime, exposes
its blackening corpse coffined within my heart.

And if I did not speak, my mouth would mutter,
would that you all would bear a sin as bitter:
I should not feel then so alone, apart.

[7 August 1935]

Sin

A hardened sinner I must be,
but this just suits me fine.
There's just one thing that bothers me:
how my sin isn't mine.

I am a sinner, that's quite plain,
but when I think I see,
my sin is something else again,
some stupid thing, maybe.

No miser seeks his lost gold-stake,
as I this sin in me;
I left a mother for its sake,
soft-hearted though I be.

Surely one day I'll find it, in
the heroes of the good,
with coffee, I'll confess the sin,
invite the neighbourhood.

I killed, I'll tell them. Don't know whom.
Perhaps my father might –
I watched his lifeblood stream and spume
one dark and clotted night.

I did it with a knife. No point
in colouring it in.
We too will drop, as stabbed men faint,
mortal in origin.

I'll tell them. And await (of course),
the busy-spirited,
watch for the thoughtful, and for those
who know the joy of dread.

And I'll see someone, whose warm eyes
signal this much: you're known:
what you say, others recognise,
and you are not alone...

But after all, perhaps my sin
is childish as the day;
the world, then, simple, minikin,
I can let out to play.

I own no God, but if He's there,
He needn't fret for me.
For I'll absolve myself, and share
this living company.

[August 1935]

120

Late Lament

I burn with ninety-six degrees of fever;
    mother, you aren't nursing me.
Beckoned, you went, lay down with my bereaver,
you loose, light girl, preferred death's company.
From lovely women, autumns soft and heady,
I strive to piece you back together, yearning;
but I am running out of time already,
    near spent out with this burning.

I'd gone to Szabadszállás, I remember,
    the last days of the wars;
for Budapest lay stricken that November,
and there was no bread in the city's stores.
I'd bought potatoes, millet tied in sacking,
I lay across a train's roof, belly-prone;
would not take 'no' until I'd got a chicken,
    but when I came, you'd gone.

You stole yourself away from me, gave over
    your warm breasts to the worms.
You comforted and chid your son and lover,
and look how lying were your sweetest terms.
You cooled my soup, you stirred it and you blew it,
'Eat up, my angel, grow up big for me...'
and now your void mouth tastes an earthy suet –
    cheating and treachery.

I should have eaten you!... it was your dinner –
    did I ask you? Must you
cripple your back with laundry, bread-winner,
and use a wooden box to set it true?
Just spank me once again, I'd be exultant,
happy because I could then strike you back!
You are no good! spitefully non-existent!
    You spoiled it all, you lack!

You, you're a bigger fraud than the deceiver
    who vows more than she gives!
You sneaked away from me, your dearest lover,
the pangs of labour and the faith that lives.
Gipsy! All that you gave, ingratiating,
you stole back in the end. Listen, I'll curse:
Mummy, you hear? the sound of a child, hating. –
    So scold me! Make it worse!

My mind is slowly clearing, slowly dawning,
    the sad old myth must die.
The child sees now how foolish is his yearning,
must learn to let his mother's love go by.
Man born of woman must be disappointed:
she will cheat him, or he her, at the last.
In struggle, or in peace, he is appointed
    to taste the self-same dust.

[1935; December 1936]

For more detail about the death of József's mother, see Zsuzsanna Ozsváth's introduction, pp.16-17.

That which your heart disguises
(for the 80th birthday of Freud)

That which your heart disguises
open your eyes and see;
that which your eye surmises
let your heart wait to be.

Desire – and all concede it –
kills all who are not dead.
But happiness, you need it
as you need daily bread.

Children, all of the living
yearn for our mother's arms;
lovemaking, or death-giving,
to wed's to take up arms.

Be like the Man of Eighty,
hunted by men with guns,
who bleeds, but in his beauty
still sires a million sons.

That old thorn, broken piercing
your sole, is long since drawn.
Now from your heart's releasing
death, too, falls and is gone.

That which your eye surmises
seize with your hand and will;
that which your heart disguises
is yours to kiss or kill.

[May 1936]

You Gave Me Childhood

You gave me childhood. Thirty winters' ageing
cannot withstand you, freeze gives way to thaw.
I can nor move nor sit. All unassuaging,
my own limbs hurl me, drag me to your door.

I hold you in my mouth, a dog her puppy,
and, lest I choke, I struggle to escape.
Each moment heaps upon me those unhappy
years that destroyed my destiny, my hope.

Feed me – I hunger. Cover me – I shiver.
Attend to me – I am a clumsy fool.
Your absence blows through me, a draught's cold river.
Command – and fear shall leave me, as you rule.

You listened, and my words gave up their ranting.
You looked at me: I let everything fall.
Make of me one not quite so unrelenting:
to live and die at my own beck and call!

My mother beat me out of doors – I lay there –
would crawl into myself, it was too late –
stone step down here and emptiness away there.
If I could sleep! I rattle on your gate.

Many men live as I do, dull, unfeeling,
out of whose eyes tears nonetheless can fall.
I love you, for without your power of healing
I'd not have learned to love myself at all.

[May 1936]

124

By the Danube

I

On the wharf's lowest step where I was sitting
I watched a melon rind drift with the flow.
I scarcely heard, drowned in my meditating,
the chatter of the surge, the quiet below.
As if poured from the dark heart in my body
the Danube ran, as grand and wise and muddy.

Like muscles of a working man – whoever
shovels, hammers, saws, works the brick-clay –
the turbid waves of the unending river
so crack, so tense, so slacken, so give way;
and motherlike it rocked and sang to me,
and washed the city's filth down to the sea.

And then a misty drizzle started splotching,
and then, as casually, it ceased to fall.
Yet still, as from a cavemouth I were watching
an endless rain, I gazed out at it all:
unchecked, the many-coloured past fell by,
as does the indifferent water from the sky.

The Danube simply flowed. As on a fecund
absent-minded mother's lap a child,
so played its little foam-floats, every second
rising in chuckles when it seemed she smiled;
on time's flood-tide they quivered, tilted, jarred,
like gravestones all akimbo in their yard.

II

I am made thus: what for a thousand ages
I've looked upon, now suddenly I see.
A flash, time's tally is wound up, the pages
a thousand ancestors have read with me.

I see what they could not in their distraction,
who delved, killed, kissed, wrought under time's duress.
And they, sunk in the matter-world of action,
see what I do not see, I must confess.

We know each other, as do joy and sorrow,
what's presentness for them is past for me.
They hold my pencil – we, together, borrow
this poem from their present memory.

III

My mother was a Kún, my father Magyar
in part, perhaps Romanian in full.
My mother's mouth gave me the sweetest nectar,
my father's mouth, the truth as beautiful.
If I but stir, they do embrace each other.
It grieves me sometimes when I think of how
time flies, decays. Such matter is my mother.
'You see when we are not! ...' they tell me now.

They speak to me, my being's patrimony,
in this my weakness, thus I may be well,
recalling that I'm greater than the many,
each of my ancestors in every cell –
I am the Ancestor, in my division
I multiply, blithely turn dam and sire,
and they achieve their double parturition,
many times many making one self fire!

I am the world, what is and what is fading,
all nations that contend on hill and plain,
I die with every conqueror, invading,
and suffer with the conquered in their pain.
My heart swells with them, the past's helpless debtor:
Árpád, Werbőczi, Dózsa and Zalán,
Romanian, Turk, Slovakian and Tatar,
gentle future of each Hungarian!

... I must have work. Would it were task sufficient
that one confess the past. The ripples of
the Danube, that is future, past, and present,
fondle and hold each other in their love.
Our forebears' struggle, with its strife and slaughter,
remembrance melts and renders into peace:
our common labours now to set in order,
were pains enough to be our masterpiece.

[June 1936]

Kún: Cumanian, Hungarian of ancient Turkish descent.
Árpád, Werbőczi, Dózsa, and Zalán: Hungarian and Bulgarian historical
figures.

Enlighten Him

Enlighten him, your child, to see:
thieves are still humanity,
witches – but basket-hawking selves.
(And barking dogs are dogs, not wolves!)
    Trafficking or philosophising,
    all mortal men turn hope to gold,
    sell coals, sell love; more enterprising,
    sell such a poem as this you hold.

And comfort him, if comfort be
that this is plain reality;
or you could hum him the new dance,
the fascist-communist romance –
    order the only *a priori*,
    and what is order if not this:
    no child is strictly necessary,
    no good should strictly be what is.

And if the child gapes at this tale,
and if he whimpers, stares, looks pale,
don't pander to him, don't concede
such theories drug his thought and deed;
    Look at the baby; sly and fickle,
    he screams for pity but, you know,
    while at the breast he'll smile and suckle,
    he'll let his teeth and sharp nails grow.

[October 1936]

Beautiful Immemorial Woman

Beautiful immemorial woman, goal of my eyes' desiring,
whose soft and fairy loveliness is sealed in her retiring,
who when we three were walking along the meadow-marges,
so seriously, so merrily, stepped in the loose mud-patches,
who when she looked at me I could not help but shiver,
beautiful immemorial woman, I would not be her lover.
I'd only like to see her, I have no plan or quarry,
sunbathing in the garden, dreaming and solitary,
and, shut up like herself, a closed book in her hand,
and all around her sighing autumn branches in the wind.
I'd gaze at her; she'd stir; and vague and dilatory,
as in a windy bower comes the whisper of a worry,
she'd stand and look about her and turn her steps away
behind the thickset bushes to the hidden passage-way
that lies in wait to lead her where I may touch her never,
and avenues of willows waving farewell forever;
as an orphan for his mother, I thirst after her sight,
beautiful immemorial woman, departing in the light.

[October 1936]

Agony

Hither, thither
from the gaze of death you dither
(mouse, frozen in its hole with terror),

while lust warms you
flee to her who guards and calms you:
woman's lap, her arms, the bearer.

Warm, enchanting,
pit of loin and cheat of wanting,
flung there by our very needing –

everybody
seeks a woman, holds her, greedy,
loves till lips are pale with kneading.

Double treasure,
double burden, pain and pleasure.
But who loves and has no lover

is as fenceless
as the beast that squats defenceless,
nature-called, no clothes or cover.

Run for shelter:
stab your mother, helter skelter,
hero of the knife, returning!

She who reads me,
understands me, never needs me,
casts me off in all my yearning.

Finest grieving:
I've no place among the living.
Head drums with the pain that rakes it;

rattle, rattle:
in the baby's hand the rattle:
left alone, he shakes and shakes it.

What requital
could repay a hurt so vital?
Probe it, shamelessly addicted:

worldly fashion
must reject the man of passion,
sun-bedazzled, dream-afflicted.

Clothes and cover
fall from off the happy lover:
culture falls from me, reveals me –

can she bear it,
watch death toss my soul and tear it
as lone torment flays and peels me?

Both the mother
and the birthing child must suffer:
twofold pang whose cure's submission.

Worse, the stinging
of the man who sells his singing:
bound to shame with no remission.

Boys unlettered!
May your eyes be burst and shattered
– help me! – when that woman passes by.

Babies dreaming,
under boots be crushed, and screaming
tell her: How I feel the agony.

Good dogs roaming,
wheels contort you wrecked and foaming,
yelp to her: How great the agony.

Mothers teeming,
may the stillborn child come streaming,
cry to her: How deep the agony.

Hale ones blooming,
may you fall and break, succumbing,
mutter to her: Know the agony.

Men, bright-flaming,
for a girl each other maiming,
don't conceal it: Ah, the agony.

Horses, gleaming,
bulls that must endure their taming,
gelded, whimper: Feel the agony.

Fishes swimming,
hooked beneath the eyes, unscreaming,
gape at her: How dumb the agony.

You the living,
all that tremble, pain-perceiving,
may you burn, by garden, mountain, tree –

where she's sleeping,
come to her charred black, and creeping,
husk to her: you made this agony.

Let her hear it:
she denied her only merit;
blithely, to a creature fleeing

hither-thither,
wandering it knows not whither,
grudged the last retreat of being.

[early November 1936]

Desolation

May insects walk upon your eye. May greenish
velvety mould befuzz your breasts. You flung
me into desolation and I vanish.
Grind up your teeth; devour your human tongue.

May your fair face like sandgrains drift and trickle.
You, who for her lap has empty void,
whose busy fingers can but pet and tickle:
may they be caught in dreary webs of weed.

This hideous desire is all your being.
You wouldn't flinch if people came to see,
and, dumbly gathered in a ring, were seeing
just who made such an evil out of me.

Whom do you squeeze now? If you have a baby,
may his sole pleasure be to turn, and turn,
you blinking at him, while about you, maybe,
full-gutted alligators flop and churn.

Supine upon this bed I lie quite numbly,
I see my eye: you look at me with it.
Die! This I wish so brutishly, so dumbly,
that I believe that I could die of it.

[November–December 1936]

My Eyes Jump In and Out...

My eyes jump in and out, I'm mad again.
When I'm like this, don't hurt me. Hold me tight.
When all I am goes cross-eyed in my brain,

don't show your fist to me: my broken sight
would never recognise it anyway.
Don't jerk me, sweet, off the void edge of the night.

Think: I have nothing left to give away,
no one to have and hold. What I called 'me'
is nothing too. I gnaw its crumbs today,

and when this poem is done it will not be...
As space is by a searchlight, I am pierced through
by naked sight: what sin is this they see

who answer not, no matter what I do,
they who by law should love, be claimed by me.
Do not believe this sin you can't construe,

till my grave-mould acquits and sets me free.

[November–December 1936]

The Scream

Love me wildly, to distraction,
scare away my huge affliction!
In the cage of an abstraction,
    I, an ape, jump up and down,
bare my teeth in malediction,
for I have no faith or fiction,
    in the terror of His frown.

Mortal, do you hear my singing,
or mere nature's echoes ringing?
Hug me, don't just stare unseeing
    as the sharpened knife comes down –
there's no guardian that's undying
who will hear my song and sighing:
    in the terror of His frown.

As a raft upon a river,
Slovak raftman, whosoever,
so the human race forever
    dumb with pain, goes drifting down –
but I scream in vain endeavour:
love me: I'll be good, I shiver
    in the terror of His frown.

[November–December 1936]

Inventory Closed

I trusted in myself from the beginning –
If nothing's there that's worth the cost of winning,
there's nothing left to lose. Our death's no heavier
than that of voiceless beasts, who cease forever.
Even in mortal fear, I kept my station –
was born, received, found individuation.
I paid each man according to his measure,
loved frankly who gave freely of his pleasure.
Woman who played with me for promised joy
I took in good faith – let her have her toy!
I swabbed the ship, jerked up the bucketful.
Among sly masters, played the stupid fool.
I sold bread, paperbacks, and toy windmills,
newspapers, poems – whichever paid the bills.
No field of victory, nor servile rope,
but a soft bed will be my end, I hope.
When, come what may, the inventory's done,
I died of life – I'm not the only one.

[November–December 1936]

Welcome for Thomas Mann (*see page 137*):
See endnotes 13 in Zsuzsanna Ozsváth's introduction, p.41.

Desző Koszytolányi (1885-1936) was one of the great Hungarian poets of the
20th century.

Welcome for Thomas Mann

Just as a tired child when put to bed
and tucked in snug, a stubborn sleepy-head,
still begs 'Don't go away, tell me a story'
(lest night should fall on him in sudden fury),
and while his little heart, congested, pants,
and even he knows not just which he wants,
the story, or your stay; may we prevail
on you to sit with us and tell a tale.
Tell us the old story, we won't forget,
how you've been with us always, will be yet,
how we are with you, an unparted whole,
whose cares are worthy of a human soul.
You know it well, the poet never lies;
tell the full truth, not only that which is,
tell of that light which flames up in our brain:
when we're apart, in darkness we remain.
As Hans Castorp through Madame Chauchat's flesh,
let us tonight see through ourselves afresh,
your words, like pillows, muffle out the din –
tell us the joy of beauty, and the pain,
lifting our hearts from mourning to desire.
We've laid poor Kosztolányi in the mire,
and on mankind, as cancer did on him,
horrible monster-states gnaw limb by limb,
and we, aghast, ask what's the next disease,
whence fall new wolvish ideologies,
what newer poison boils within our blood –
how long, and where, you can still read aloud?...
So. When you speak, we must not lose our flame,
we men should still be men in more than name,
and women still be women – lovely, free –
because true humans daily cease to be...
Sit down. Start our favourite story – please.
We'll listen; happy he who only sees
your face among our race of evil will,
to know there's one true European still.

[early January 1937]

Ars Poetica

(for Andor Németh)

Then why should I, a poet, study
poetry? The wet star, that eye
which swims upon the midnight eddy,
may not with grace ascend the sky.

Time oozes down, and I no longer
suck the breast milk of fairytales;
I quaff the real world in my hunger,
whose foamy head is heaven's pales.

To swim that lovely spring's surprises!
Silence and quivering embrace,
and from the white foam there arises
a fluent chatter, wit, and grace.

Those other poets – why should I worry
how they defile their paunch and crop?
with gin and trumped-up imagery
let them feign drunkenness, throw up.

I leap the time's saloon, its liquor,
strive for intelligence, and beyond!
My brain is free, I'll not play sucker
and serve their fatuous demi-monde.

Let nature be your test and measure!
Let yourself eat, drink, sleep, embrace!
No pain shall make me serve the pleasure
of powers so crippling, vile, and base.

No bargains – peace of mind is better! –
lest all the world should see my shame,
my skin marked by its scarlet tetter,
my juice drunk up by fever's flame.

I shan't stop my litigious clamour.
I plead my case to the clear mind.
I am the age's guide and grammar,
the ploughman hears me at his grind.

The worker's body feels me, only
between two motions stiff with pain;
the ill-dressed lout waits for me, lonely,
outside the movie, in the night rain.

As for the entrenched scum, who injure
my poems' form to please the times:
brotherly tanks are my avenger,
rumbling out my powerful rhymes.

Mankind is not yet grown, I'm saying.
But he aspires, and thus he's wild.
His parents – thought, and love undying –
may they watch over their lost child.

[early February 1937]

Andor Németh was one of József's oldest and best friends.

Flóra

1 *Hexameters*

Mushy, the snow is collapsing, the tin-mutter guttering dribbles,
slush-packs, blackening, swoon and sublime, their substances vanish,
bubbling fluid makes ruffles, and gushes, and slides for the culvert;
airlight, the brightness dissolves, betrembles the heavenly arches,
and rosily joyful desire is shedding its shirt on the dawnscape.

See then how much, how frighted-from-swoon I adore you, Flóra!
Now in this chattering lovely meltworld the grief of my heart you
dissolve, as a bandage is washed from a scar – and I tingle with
                        quickening.
Listen: your name is a floodtide eternal, a delicate brightness,
a charm, and I shiver to think how I could have existed without you.

2 *Mysteries*

I, as in a fairytale,
at the call of mystery
come to attention, don the mail
of head-to-toe fidelity.

Breezes sing and waters cry,
blushes tell you understand:
speakings of the heart and eye
flow in a single mild command.

Since it seems that I adore you,
and this song chimes in with theirs:
this great faith, thus I implore you,
share the burden that it bears.

József met Flóra on 20 February 1937. He composed this series of poems in
the course of the next few days. For more detail on this relationship, see
Zsuzsanna Ozsváth's introduction, pp.37-38.

3 *Two Billion Now*

Two billion people seek to bind me fast
to be their tool and loyal animal.
Beauty and kindness, weary now at last,
move southwards, to a home more natural.
To hold that world up to the light of being,
the culture-dish the doctor frowns at seeing,
I am unable, I surrender, fleeing,
if you don't help me, love, to bear it all.

You're needed as the peasant needs the soil,
the silent rain, the purifying sun.
You're needed like the greenness of the cell
swelling the leafbloom that the plant has spun.
You're needed as the working folk who hunger,
in trembling labour and in helpless anger
to birth the future, and can wait no longer,
need work, bread, freedom, words that make us one.

I need you, Flóra, as the villages
need bricks, electric lights; need wells and schools;
as children toys, protection, families,
as workers consciousness, the human tools.
And in this topsy-turvy world, this madness,
the brain needs pattern, as the poor need goodness,
a bright light in the tangle of our sadness,
to point it to itself and guide its rules.

4 *Aspiration*

So were my love matched by my aspiration,
and peace might come to humankind in sooth,
then I'd search out in heartfelt dedication
the source,
the very fountain of eternal youth.

My burdened soul's now joyful only under
the red dawn where unfolds the first green growth –
even the branch that waves farewell…this wonder
I seek,
the fabled fountain of eternal youth.

Let the tongued sciences observe and chatter –
whoever sees in me my heart's pure truth
would succour my desire in this great matter,
for what
is not: the fountain of eternal youth.

5 *Be Measured!*

No ghost-house on a vacant holding
my soul is now, but bravely building;
for, sick with phantoms null and yielding,
Flóra I found, my all-enfolding:

she, the dew upon the grasses,
truth, where a dubious shadow passes,
tramples my nightmare serpents' faces,
washes with smiles my sorrows' traces.

Simple water is amazing:
pure as water tastes her kissing;
she calls me home from bullies' chasing,
in her eyes a pony grazing.

She is the charter wherein gladness
pleads with the dust and void of sadness,
my anxious love against the deadness,
spirit's argument with madness.

Through my inmost thoughts you've ranged me;
a rash man, to a brave you changed me,
suffered till you loved and named me,
and became the sky that framed me.

Hail to you, announced and treasured,
love me, always be remembered,
and, lest your praise be lost or beggared,
thus forever you are measured.

[February 1937]

142

March

1

The luke rain sprinkles faint and fainter,
a downy beardlet greens the wheat.
As storks seek chimneys, so the winter
finds out the mountains in defeat.
Now bursts the jubilance of strife
in green explosions, airy, vernal,
and from the carpentry of life
waft piny scents of hope eternal.

What's in the papers? Rape and pillage:
thugs in the noble fields of Spain;
the Chinese serfs driven from their village
by a brute warlord, who'll regain
their ancient holdings; armies loom,
the tortured poor groan in their body
beneath their clownish tyrants' doom,
and linen, white, is drenched and bloody.

Happy am I, a child's my spirit
in Flóra's love. But, treachery,
against our sweet love's naked merit
march tanks and iron and worse, for see:
the basest of humanity.
Life's future is the only freeing;
against their cruel intensity
my only refuge is our being.

2

I fear them, for it's necessary:
paid killers as they are, paid tarts.
The woman-whore, man-mercenary,
I cannot reach their alien hearts.
My life is all I have, the brain,
careful and practical, is learning.
While the hurt world cools in its pain,
my Flóra's heart and mine are burning.

For we'll beget a girl so pretty,
clever and good; a brave wise boy;
they'll save a shred of us, our pity,
like sunfire from the Milky Way, –
and when the Sun is guttering,
our princelings in their sweet machines
shall fly, and fearless, chattering,
find stars to plough the earthly genes.

[March 1937]

Tumble out of the Flood

Terrify me, my hidden God,
I need your wrath, your scourge, your thunder;
quick, come tumble out of the flood,
lest nothingness sweep us asunder.

I am the one the horse knocks down,
up to my eyes in dirt, a cipher,
and yet I play with knives of pain
too monstrous for man's heart to suffer.

How easily I flame! the sun
is not more prone to burn – be frightening,
scream at me: leave the fire alone!
Rap my hands with your bolt of lightning.

Hammer it into me with rage
or grace: it's innocence that's evil!
that innocence could be my cage
burns at me fiercer than a devil.

A fragment from a wreck I lie,
tossed by a cruel tempest frothing;
alone; I dare, and I defy:
all merely signifying nothing.

144

I'd choke my very breath, to die,
your rod and staff thus disobeying,
and look you boldly in the eye,
you empty, human-faced unbeing!

[March 1937]

To Flóra

Without your love I would be driven
to give back what I have been given:
to douse these coals that cost so dear,
close the tired eyes I open here.

It's good to die. No love, no tether
to tie me and the world together.
Beside that green, that white-legged sky,
those clouds of chattering stars, I'd lie,

by the far shore of tranquillity,
the coastline of all non-nullity,
and watch the universes be
like flowers upon a flowering tree.

A cabin-boy, amid the clatter
of the old towing-boat, the *Tatar*,
a lovely summer's day I spent
like one who's learned what pleasure meant;

I watched the Danube's drift and tumble
so set a leafy branch to tremble
that rings of ruffles spread abroad;
the brown tide nibbled beam and board,

carried more golden melon-parings
than you'd believe in twenty hearings,
more than I would myself believe,
but you I never would deceive.

Red apples likewise rocked and jiggled,
green peppers limped and swam and wriggled;
you'd hunger after this or that,
and the ship nodded, tipped its hat.

That's how it looks from far out yonder.
So beautiful! – I'd nod, and ponder
just how the sky can blaze so blue
and what a perfect fit for you.

Because the cosmos is a bonus,
gives more than is its due or onus,
life overflows death's final shore,
whelms the heart's margins in its roar,

height, depth, silence's frontier,
just as the great Danube did that year...
I have your love, I sleep in peace,
therefore I safely can confess:

caught likewise at the edge of being,
I never matched whom I was playing;
my soul's thus common property:
that's why I love you so, you see.

[March 1937]

'Tatár' was the name of the tug-boat aboard which József worked
as a deck-hand in the summer of 1919.

For My Birthday

Upon my thirty-second year –
what a surprise, this poem here,
    knicky-
    knacky:

a little gift with which I say,
lurking alone in this café:
    happy
    happy.

Thirty-two years just blew away,
I never made ten doits a day:
    hungry,
    Hungary.

A pedagogue I might have been,
not this pen-busting, might-have-been,
    saddie
    laddie.

But no; Herr College Chancellor
showed me the outside of the door:
    mocktor
    Doktor.

It was a short sharp shock for sure,
my 'father' poem got its cure;
    his word
    and sword,

that saved the fatherland from me,
evoked my spirit and set free
    its name
    and flame.

'As long as I have any say
you'll not teach here a single day' –
    bibble-
    babble.

If Mr Antal Horger's pleased
our poet's grammar-study's ceased –
  folly's
  jollies –

no high school, but a nation I,
although he like not, by and by
  shall teach,
  shall teach.

[11 April 1937]

On the Antal Horger affair, see Zsuzsanna Ozsváth's introduction, pp.17-18.

(Here comes the storm...)

Here comes the storm, ebony foaming,
judges in black, their angry gloaming
split by the lightnings' zigzag roaming,
like headache's sickening missiles,
followed by velvety rustles,
the jasmine's trembling vessels.

Apple-petals – branch yet unshattered –
strive to untie, for flight unfettered,
little moth-wings – as if it mattered!
The grassblades all droop and shiver,
up the soft slope from the river,
fear that the darkfall's forever.

They shake an undreamed accusation –
The little ones give demonstration
how you should bear pain's desolation:
give it such melody to the ear
that if the grass itself should hear,
then you would grass to grass appear.

[May 1937]

148

My Country

1

As I walked home I felt a looming,
a velvet rustle sway and pause:
within that warm and wafty gloaming
the jasmines gave their soft applause.

My heart was a great jungle, dreaming,
and people slept in streets and doors.
What fed my power of thought and naming
then struck me, with its root and cause.

It was community, our brother,
this poor, drunk comrade called the other,
this bosom-giving nature, who

curses in somber working-places
or through night's huge tree-hollow spaces
sits brooding in the nation's woe.

2

A thousand epidemics raging,
unchecked infant mortality,
orphanings, early death by aging,
madness and infertility,

suicide, sin, that inner hedging,
waiting for miracles aimlessly, –
too late to stop the haemorrhaging,
already now we should be free!

The working people could have met,
in expert, wise deliberation,
to thrash our troubles out with grace.

The present governors of our nation,
becharmed with violence, forget
how perishes our lovely race!

3

The workman deadlifts stump and silage
and earns a hernia for his pains,
the landlord razes house and village,
his axes turn the woods to plains.

That brave man who with skill and knowledge
rescued his land from fires and rains
is driven like a beast of tillage
to vote for all-wise suzerains.

The gendarmes' plumes so kitty-pretty
smile in the country and the city
and seal and sign the voters' choice,

"free" voters who millennially
bound to themselves like sheaves of barley
smirk and obey their master's voice.

4

Our lords were neither dull nor feeble,
but held their lands against our claim,
one and a half million people
reeled to America in shame.

His heart was tight, his legs unable,
he vanished on the cruel seafoam;
like one whose sins he drowns in tipple
he vomited, remembered home.

One man still heard the cowbell's babble:
his neighbour knew that such a dupe
would not keep food upon the table.

Our past is packed and bundled up,
and like the immigrant, heartsore,
we too await a new world's shore.

5

The workers' wage no further stretches
than one man's soup and one man's bread,
and wine-and-fizz, so the poor wretches
yell and sing out to wake the dead.

The country's interest never reaches
to why they let these problems breed:
industry starved, the nation's riches
wasted when workers are in need.

The weaver dreams of cake and icing,
knows not the great cartels' devising.
She clutches, Saturdays, her money,

docked by a fine – 'it's almost funny,'
her shilling grins in silent mirth:
'I show how much your work is worth.'

6

The rich look on the poor with horror,
the poor look on the rich with dread.
We're driven by a crafty terror,
our hope, delusory, is dead.

The peasant's rights fare all the poorer
with eaters of the peasant's bread,
the hired man rots like straw, when clearer
demands might have been credited.

A thousand years he has been coming,
the people's son, the people roaming,
a little bundle on a stave.

A janitor's cap is his ambition,
buying his wretched manumission
to flog with sticks his father's grave.

7

Yet still my soul cries out in danger,
as alien to its Magyar kin,
dear country, hold me not a stranger,
true son of a true origin!

A chained, lug-headed bear, a cringer,
the folk takes what for me were sin!
Call off your bailiffs, lest they injure
the pinion of my poet's pen!

You gave your landsmen to the ocean;
give back humanity to men.
Let Magyars know their true devotion

and not the German regimen.
Give good and true their proper motion
within my poet's song again.

[May 1937]

section 4: József alludes here to the late 19th and early 20th century emigration of over one million of the Hungarian agrarian proletariat and poor peasantry to the United States.

section 7: József was aware of and deeply troubled by the influence of the Third Reich on Hungary.

(Who would this poem...)

Who would this poem's reader be,
must know its poet, must love me,
sailing upon the vacuum,
knowing, as seers do, what's to come;

for he has dreamed, thus fathomless,
in human form a quietness,
and in his heart will come and go
the tiger and the gentle doe.

[early June 1937]

Eagle

Eagle, gigantic, diving
heaven's echoey precipices!
What winged thing's this, arriving
from voids and nothingnesses!

His starry beak of azure
devours the vaulted cosm,
his talons of erasure
rip at its flesh-warm bosom.

The world's eyeball, transparent,
weeps at the the bloody capture,
the downy feathers errant.
This is the red dawn's rapture.

There is no height above it,
essence is torn and savaged;
there is no depth beneath it,
being itself is ravished.

One wing is my own aura,
the other wing is Flóra:
newborn, beyond all seeming,
each thus in each redeeming.

[June 1937]

Mercy Denied Forever

Mercy denied forever,
pain's but a vain endeavour,
be what you should be: manly.
Grass in your footsteps ever.

Sin is beyond endurance,
weeping, vain self-abhorrence.
Even for this, be grateful,
warrant for your existence.

Renounce self-flagellations,
promises, accusations,
both conquest and surrender,
the call of crowds and nations.

Avoid another's uses,
nor spy into abuses.
And do not scorn the human:
you are what it produces.

You begged for pity, croaking,
in vain, remember, choking,
and bore yourself false witness
in your own trial's convoking.

You sought a father, even
on earth, if not in heaven.
In Freud the wicked children
you found, still unforgiven.

You trusted words' illusions,
paid comforters' delusions,
but no one ever trusted
the goodness of your visions.

They loved you by their lying,
your lying killed your loving,
therefore the pistol-barrel
aimed at your blank heart dying.

Or cast out doctrine's power,
hope true love yet will flower,
doglike, you'd trust whoever
trusted you for an hour.

[June 1937]

'On Our Poet and His Time'
(for Bertalan Hatvany)

Here's my poem, with the title
'On Our Poet and His Time'.
'O' begins its full recital,
'rhyme' will be its second rhyme.
Nothingness so flits within it
as a something's dust, a minute
past its prime...

Nothingness so flits and dances
as if it a something were;
universe expands, condenses
to the future, floating there;
space, the sea, the branched tree-branches,
dogs whose howling avalanches,
sing its sphere...

I, my chair, each fry and phylum,
and the Earth beneath the Sun,
solar system, this asylum,
with the galaxies strive on –
cosmos plunges into zero
as, contrariwise, your hero,
here begun...

Space is my soul. And to its mother,
that great Space, it fain would fly.
Balloon to gondola, I tether
soul to body, to make I.
As neurotic sublimation
this my truth, or dream and vision,
they deny...

Come, my friend, let's face existence.
You must work here on the ground.
Empathy's become resistance.
Your wild fables are unsound.
Leave the former, leave the latter,
watch the twilight colours scatter,
melting round...

Red blood steeps the fields of stubble,
distant moors congeal to blue.
Grassy meadows sag with trouble,
softly cry as if they knew.
On the cheerful hillocks falling
death's lividity is crawling.
Evening dew.

[late August 1937]

Bertalan Hatvany (1900-80) financed *The Luminous Word*; he also supported
Attila József regularly for many years.

156

(No flowers, but a spike...)

No flowers, but a spike, you proffered,
scorn to the other world you offered,
gold you promised her who suffered,
her, your mother; now you squat,

mad toadstool in the roots, and glower
(appear thus to your anxious knower),
locked up inside the Seven Tower,
where hope is void, escape is not.

With milk teeth, why did you bite granite?
Your daydream errand, why begin it?
Why, too late, try to save a minute?
What did you want then, after all?

Your nakedness you always flaunted,
tore off the scabs from wounds you vaunted,
you're famous, if that's what you wanted.
And have you done your time? You fool.

Did you give love? Who would embrace you?
Fugitive! who would even chase you?
Just make the best of what will face you:
no breadknife, and of course no bread.

You're in the Seven Tower for good.
Be glad if you have firewood,
glad for a pillow to your bed,
be a good boy, lay down your head.

[November 1937]

Seven Tower: See details in Zsuzsanna Ozsváth's Introduction, p.39.

(And so I've found my native country...)

And so I've found my native country,
that soil the gravedigger will frame,
where they who write the words above me
do not for once misspell my name.

This black collection-box receives me
(for no one needs me any more),
this Iron Six that was worth twenty,
this coin left over from the war.

None needs that iron ring inscripted
with sweet words, that the world is new:
rights, land. – Our laws are the leftovers;
now pretty gold rings all pursue.

For many years I had been lonely.
Then many people visited.
I'd have been happy if they'd stayed.
You are alone, was what they said.

And so I lived, useless and empty,
and now I see it all quite plain.
They let me play the fool until
by now even my death's in vain.

All through my life I've tried to weather
the whirlwind that would always blow.
I was more sinned against than sinning,
and it's a laugh that it was so.

Spring, summer, autumn, all are lovely;
but winter's loveliest for one
who hopes for hearth and home and family
only for others, when all's done.

[24 November 1937]

This is József's last poem.

Zsuzsanna Ozsváth and Frederick Turner have also translated Miklós Radnóti, one of the great Hungarian poets of the 20th century, and received Hungary's most prestigious literary award, the Milán Füst Prize of the Hungarian Academy of Sciences, for their translation, *Foamy Sky: The Major Poems of Miklós Radnóti* (Princeton University Press, 1992). As well as being Professor of Literature and the History of Ideas in the School of Arts and Humanities at the University of Texas at Dallas, she is the Director of the School's Holocaust Studies Program. Born in the former Yugoslavia, she grew up in Hungary, leaving the country in 1957 after the defeated revolution. Her work focusses on aesthetic and ethical dilemmas, Holocaust literature and translations from German and Hungarian. A recipient of several prestigious literary awards, she has published in a wide variety of journals, such as *Judaism, The Partisan Review, German Studies Review, The Hungarian Quarterly* and *Research Studies*.

Frederick Turner is Founders Professor of Arts and Humanities at the University of Texas at Dallas. He is a poet, interdisciplinary scholar, aesthetician, essayist, cultural critic and translator. Born in Northamptonshire in 1943 to the anthropologists Victor W. and Edith L.B. Turner, he grew up in Central Africa. He read English Language and Literature at Oxford, and his dissertation, *Shakespeare and the Nature of Time*, was published by the Clarendon Press. He has taught at the University of California at Santa Barbara, and at Kenyon College, where he was editor of the *Kenyon Review*. A winner of the Levinson Poetry Prize (and of the Milán Füst Prize with Zsuzsanna Ozsváth), he is the author of 20 books, including *Natural Classicism: Essays on Literature and Science; Genesis: an Epic Poem; Rebirth of Value: Meditations on Beauty, Ecology, Religion and Education; Beauty: the Value of Values; April Wind and Other Poems; The Culture of Hope*; and *Hadean Eclogues*.